FOUR EYES

VOLUME ONE

FORGED IN FLAMES

WRITER
JOE KELLY

ILLUSTRATOR
MAX FIUMARA

COLORIST
NESTOR PEREYRA

LETTERING & DESIGN
DREW GILL

Created by
Joe Kelly & Max Fiumara

FOUR EYES, VOL. 1: FORGED IN FLAMES

First Edition. July 2010. Published by Image Comics, Inc.

Office of publication: 2134 Allston Way, Second Floor, Berkeley, California 94704.

Copyright © 2010 Joe Kelly & Max Fiumara. All rights reserved.

Four Eyes™, its logo, and the likenesses of all characters featured herein are trademarks of Joe Kelly & Max Fiumara, unless otherwise expressly noted. Originally published in single magazine format as Four Eyes #1-4. Image Comics is a registered trademark of Image Comics, Inc. No part of this publication may be reproduced or transmitted, in any form or by any means (except for short excerpts for review purposes), without the express written permission of Joe Kelly & Max Fiumara or Image Comics, Inc. All names, characters, events, and locales in this publication are entirely fictional. Any resemblance to actual persons (living or dead), events or places, without satiric intent, is coincidental.

Printed in the U.S.A. For information regarding the CPSIA on this printed material call: 203-595-3636 and provide reference # EAST – 66825

International Rights Representative: Christine Meyer - christine@gfloystudio.com

ISBN: 978-1-60706-292-9

MAN OF action STUDIOS

WWW.MANOFACTION.TV

IMAGE COMICS, INC.
Robert Kirkman — Chief Operating Officer
Erik Larsen — Chief Financial Officer
Todd McFarlane — President
Marc Silvestri — Chief Executive Officer
Jim Valentino — Vice-President

Eric Stephenson — Publisher
Todd Martinez — Sales & Licensing Coordinator
Betsy Gomez — PR & Marketing Coordinator
Branwyn Bigglestone — Accounts Manager
Sarah deLaine — Administrative Assistant
Tyler Shainline — Production Manager
Drew Gill — Art Director
Jonathan Chan — Production Artist
Monica Howard — Production Artist
Vincent Kukua — Production Artist
Kevin Yuen — Production Artist
www.imagecomics.com

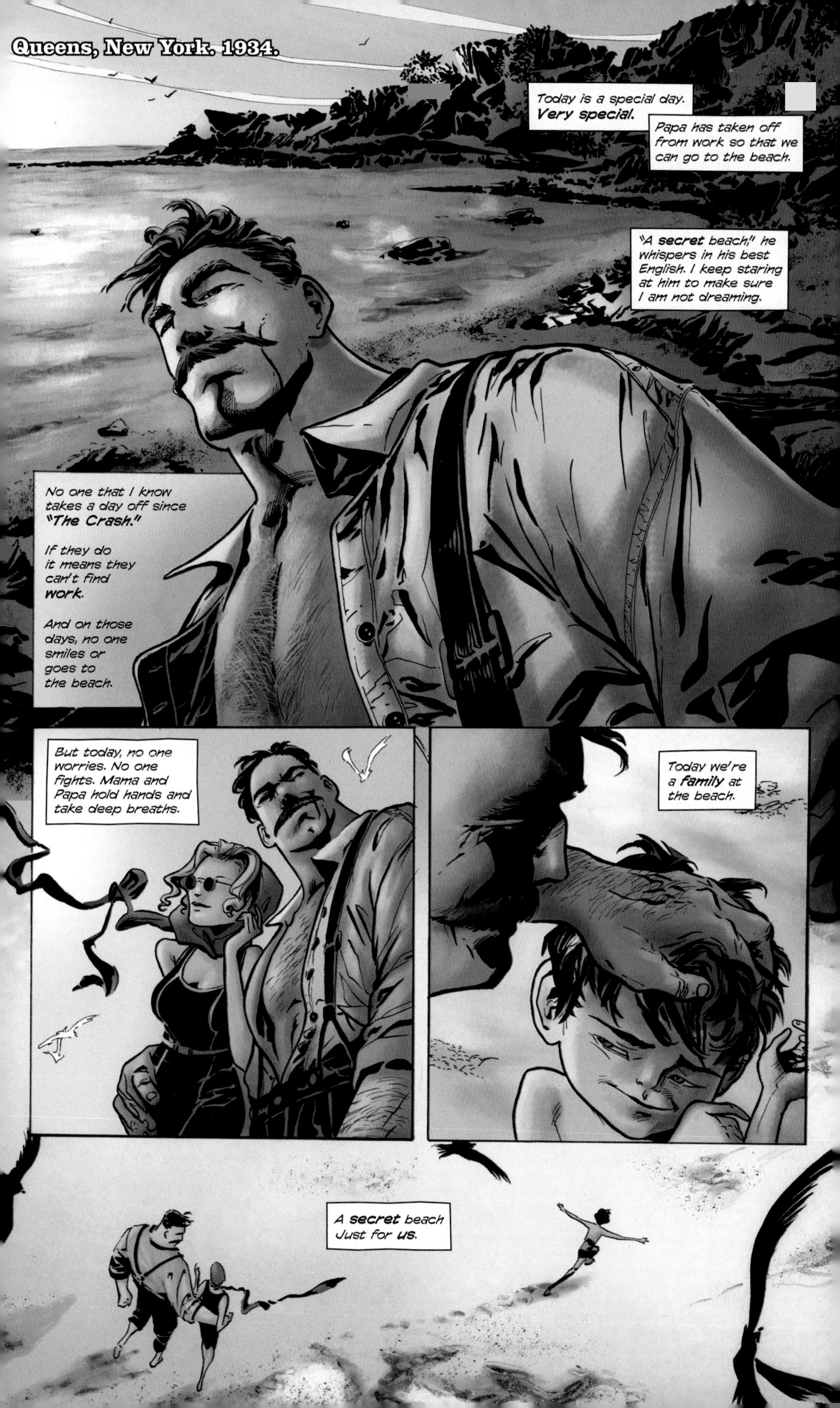
Queens, New York. 1934.
Today is a special day. **Very special.**
Papa has taken off from work so that we can go to the beach.
"A **secret** beach," he whispers in his best English. I keep staring at him to make sure I am not dreaming.
No one that I know takes a day off since **"The Crash."**
If they do it means they can't find **work**.
And on those days, no one smiles or goes to the beach.
But today, no one worries. No one fights. Mama and Papa hold hands and take deep breaths.
Today we're a **family** at the beach.
A **secret** beach Just for **us**.

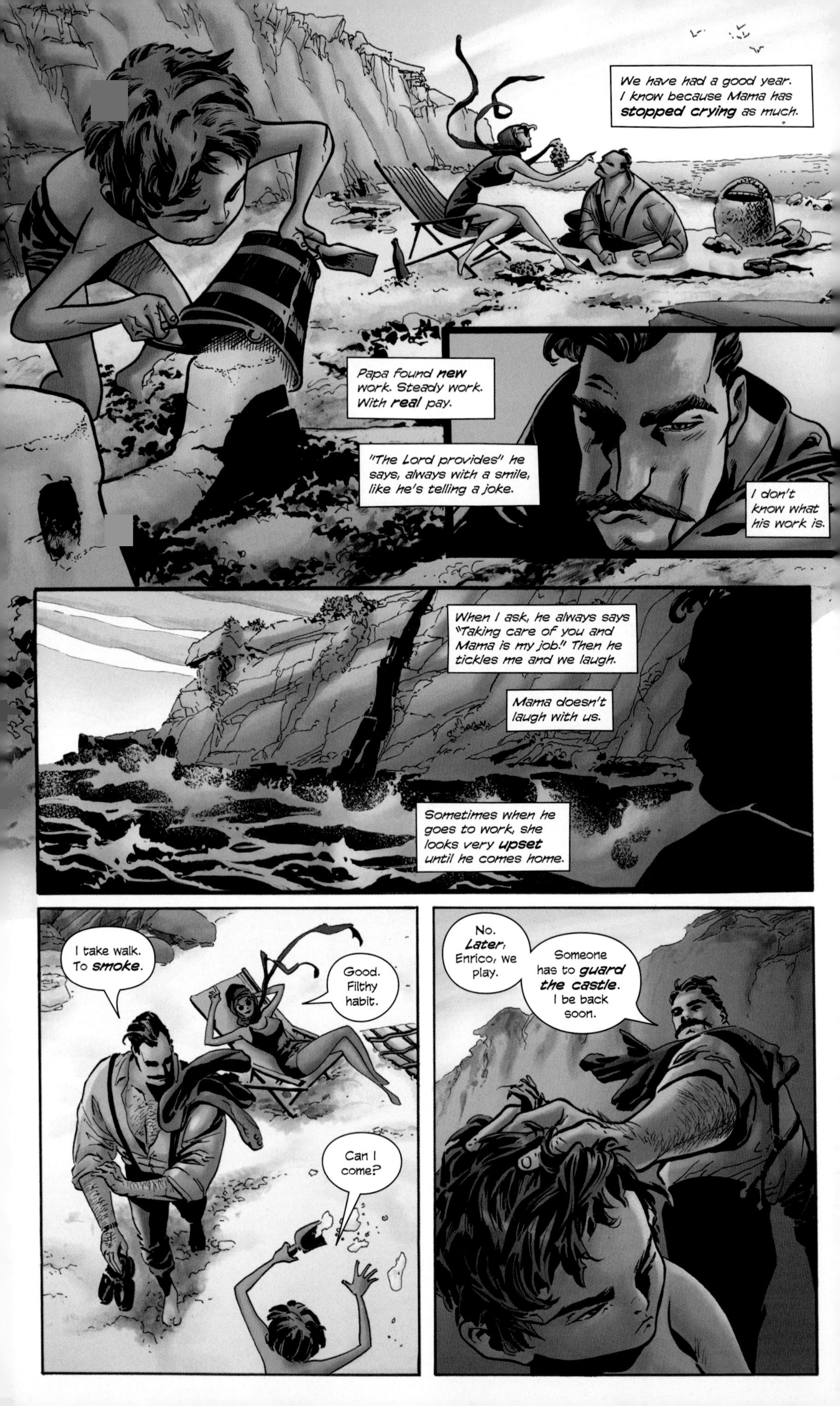
We have had a good year. I know because Mama has **stopped crying** as much.
Papa found **new** work. Steady work. With **real** pay.
"The Lord provides" he says, always with a smile, like he's telling a joke.
I don't know what his work is.
When I ask, he always says "Taking care of you and Mama is my job." Then he tickles me and we laugh.
Mama doesn't laugh with us.
Sometimes when he goes to work, she looks very **upset** until he comes home.
I take walk. To **smoke**.
Good. Filthy habit.
Can I come?
No. *Later*, Enrico, we play.
Someone has to **guard the castle**. I be back soon.

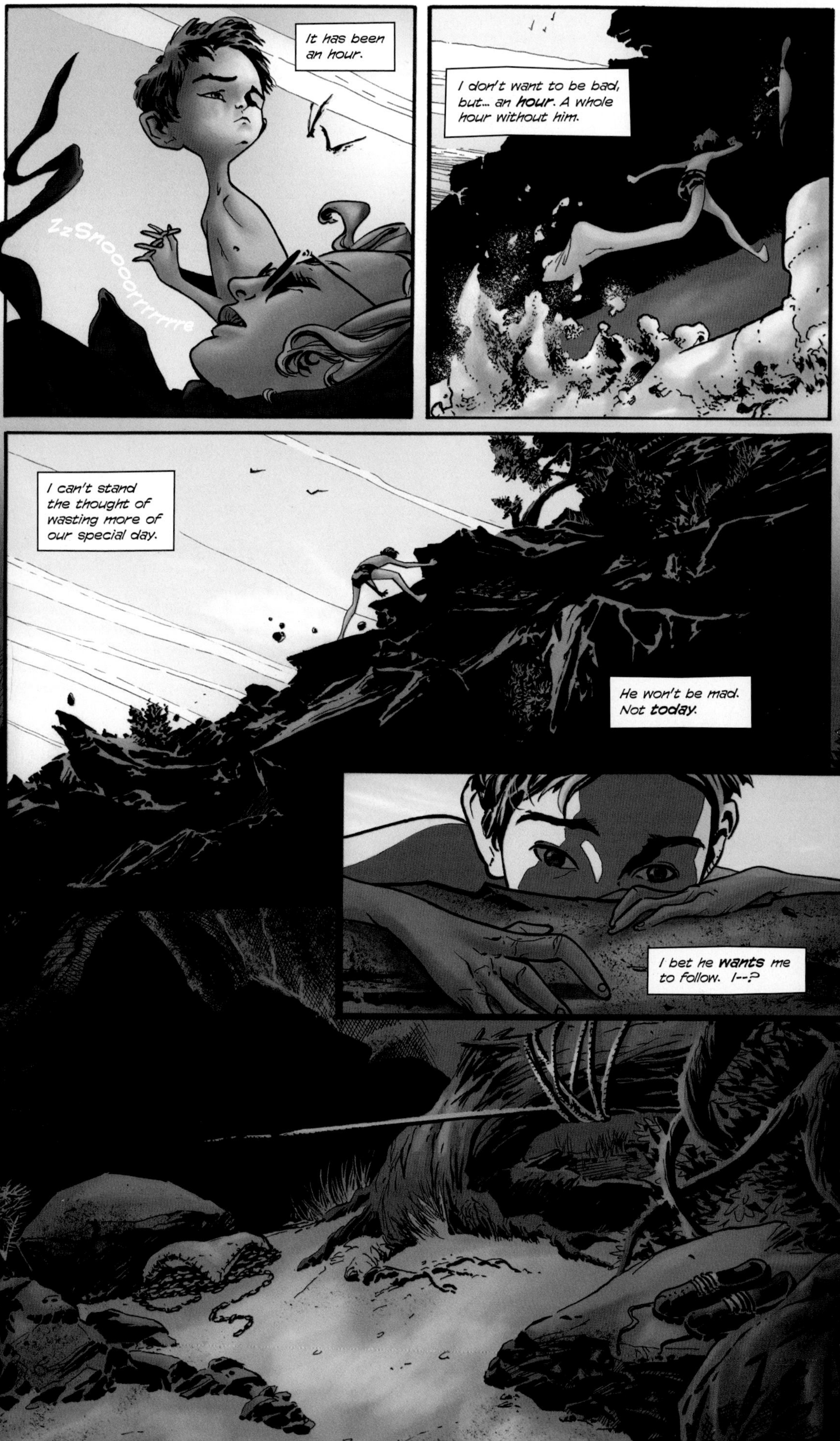
It has been an hour.
ZzSnoooorrrrrrre
I don't want to be bad, but... an **hour**. A whole hour without him.
I can't stand the thought of wasting more of our special day.
He won't be mad. Not **today**.
I bet he **wants** me to follow. I--?

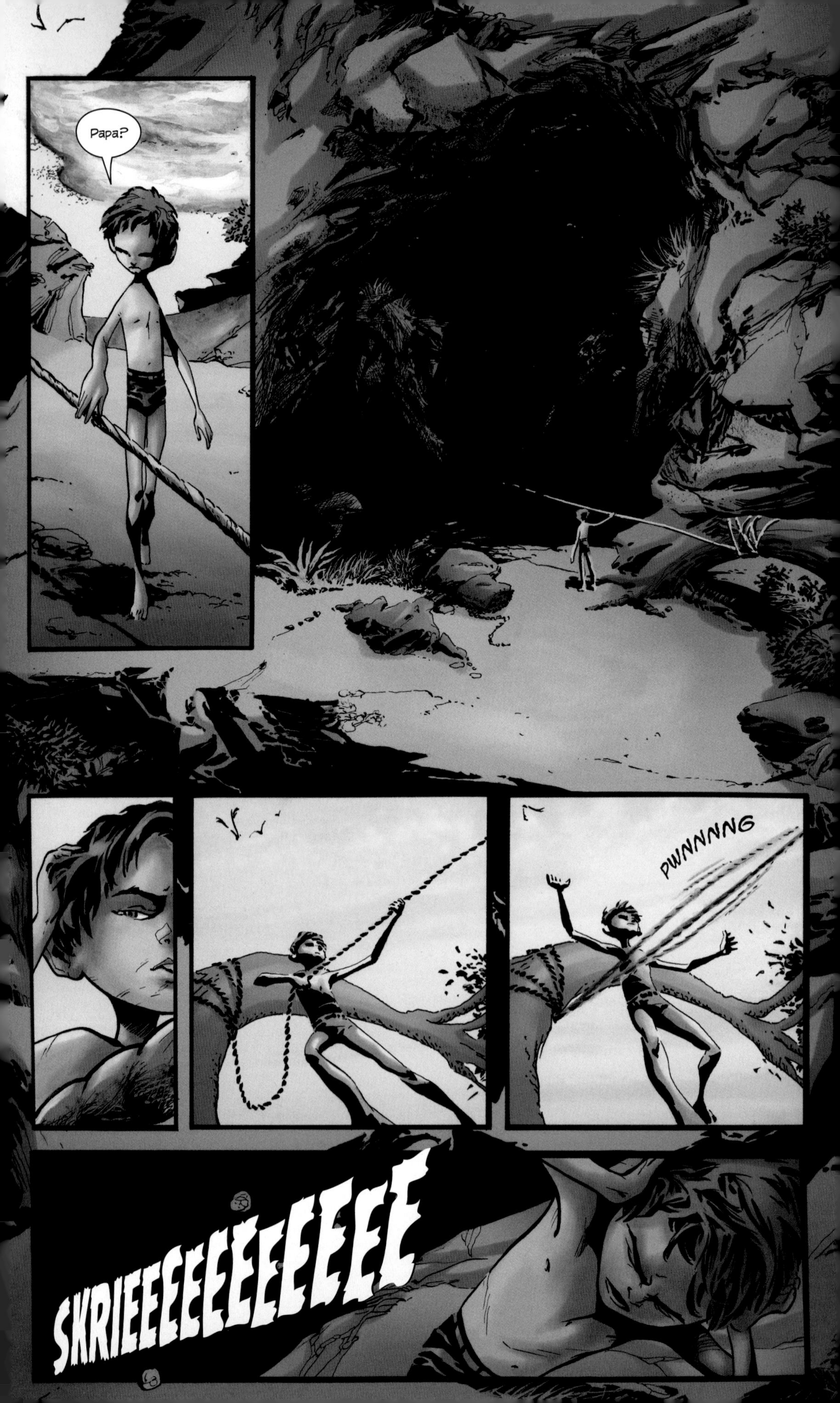
Papa?
PWNNNNG
SKRIEEEEEEEEEEEE

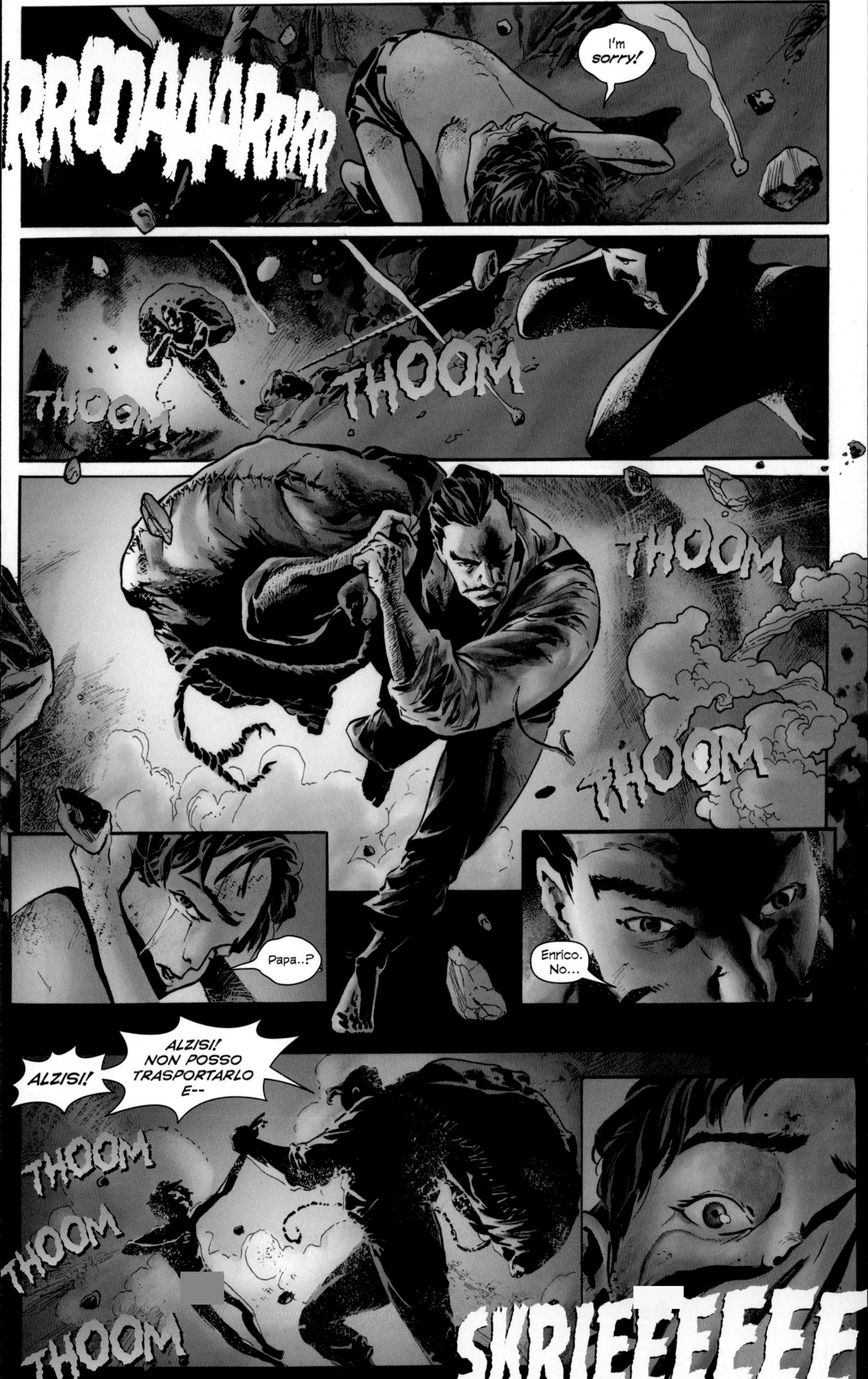
RROOAAARRRR
I'm sorry!
THOOM
THOOM
THOOM
THOOM
Papa..?
Enrico. No...
ALZISI!
ALZISI! NON POSSO TRASPORTARLO E--
THOOM
THOOM
THOOM
SKRIEEEEEE

SKRAHHHHH

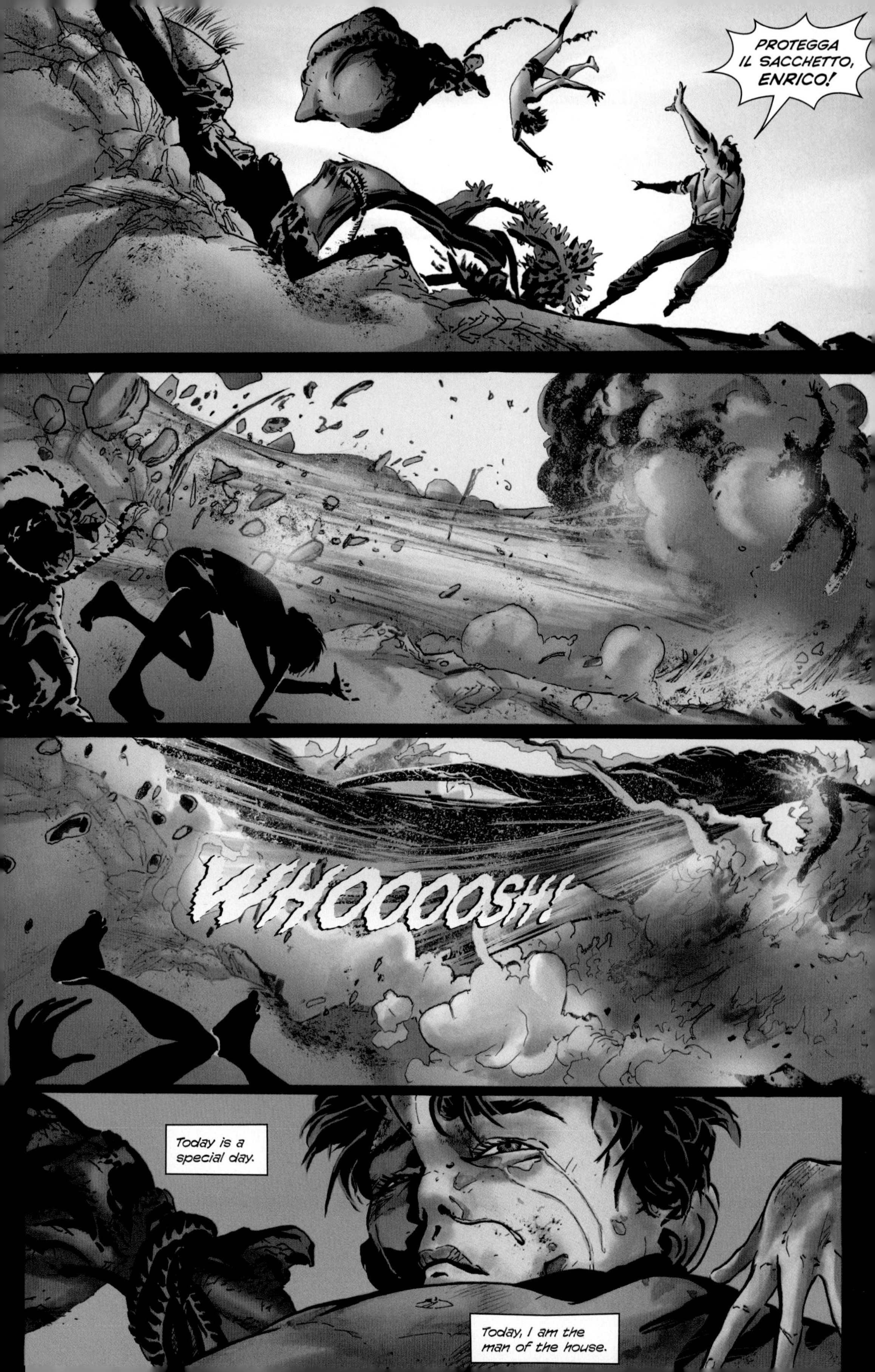
PROTEGGA IL SACCHETTO, ENRICO!
WHOOOOSH!
Today is a special day.
Today, I am the man of the house.

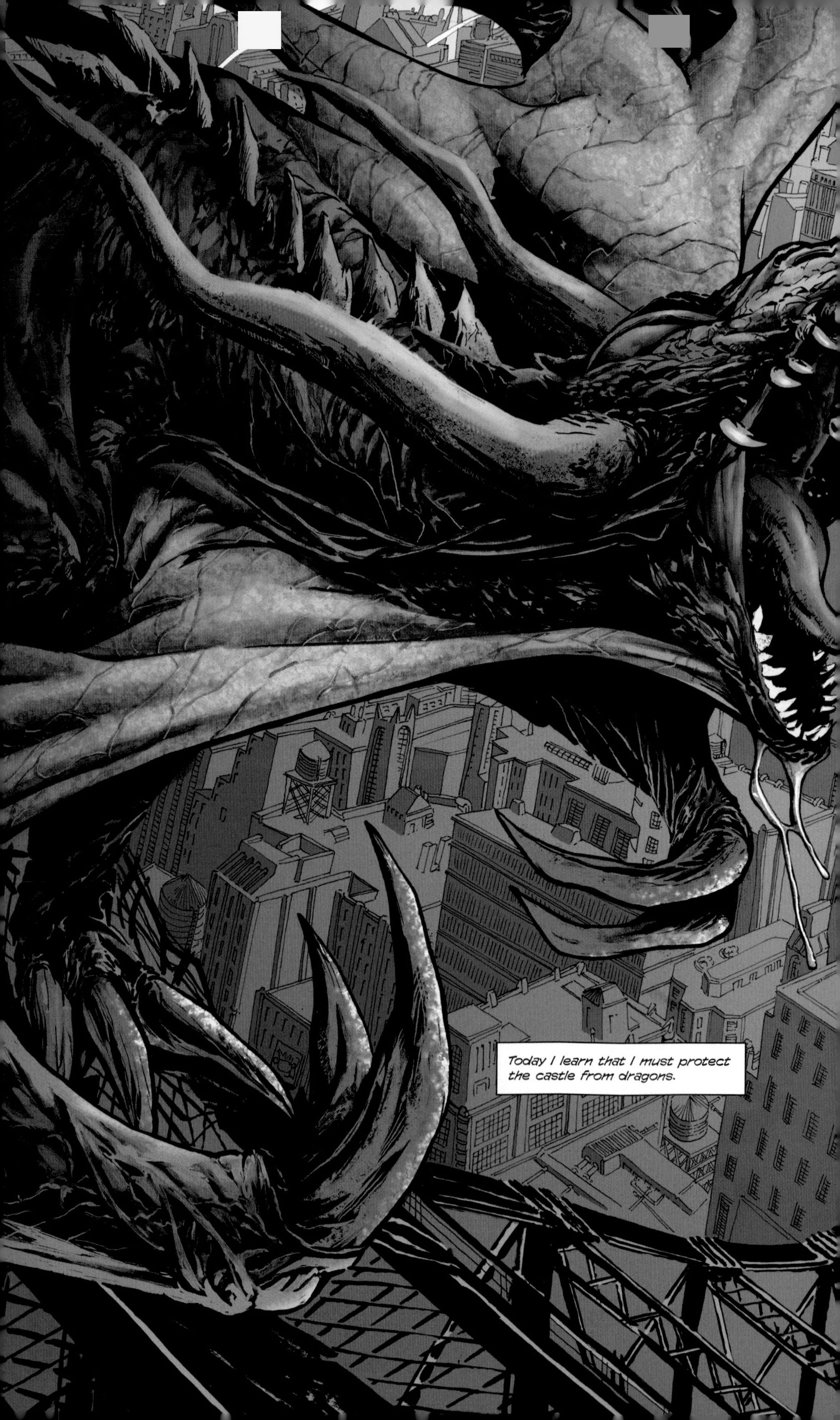
Today I learn that I must protect the castle from dragons.

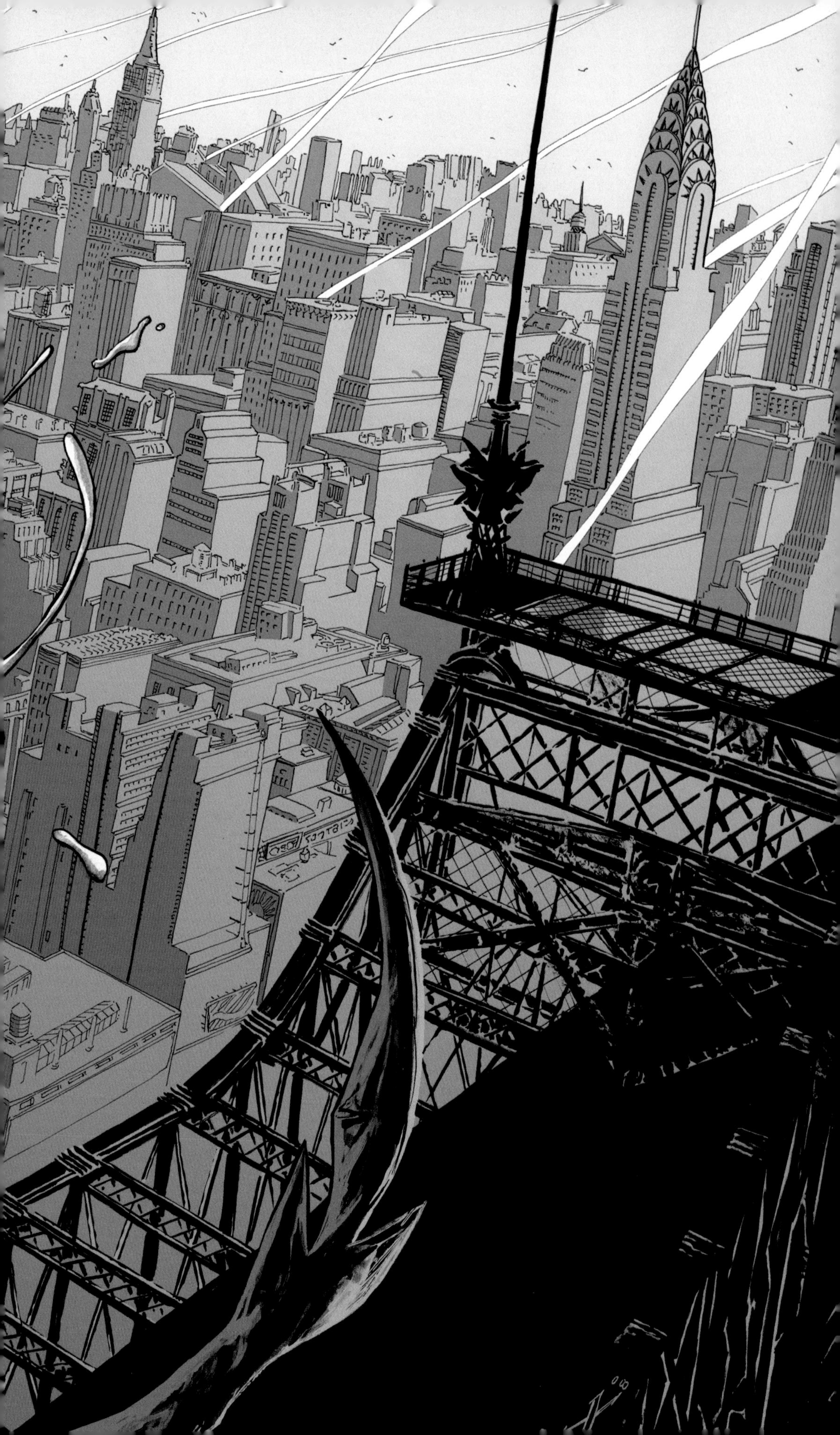

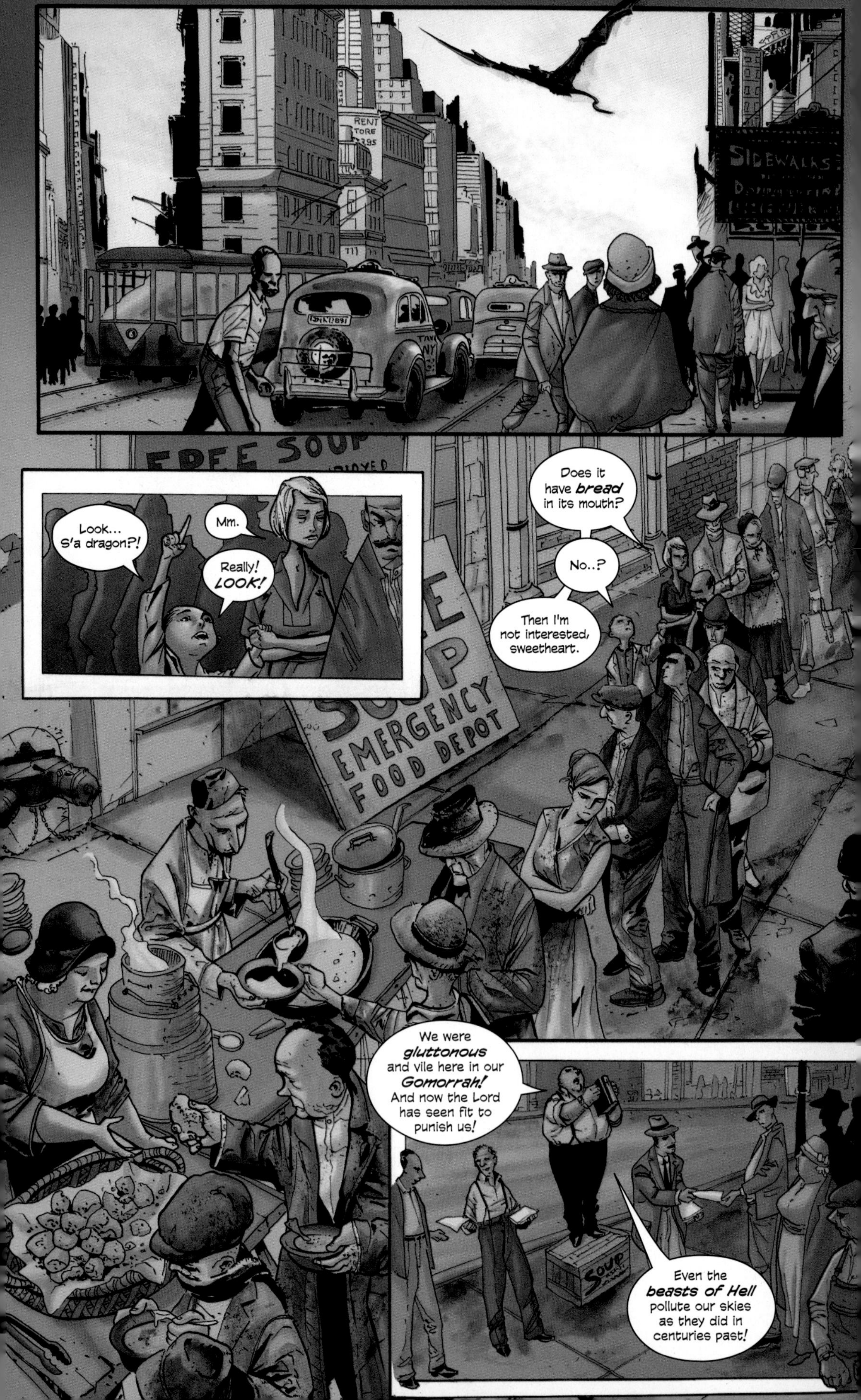

SIDEWALKS
FREE SOUP
Look... S'a dragon?!
Mm.
Really! LOOK!
Does it have bread in its mouth?
No..?
Then I'm not interested, sweetheart.
EMERGENCY FOOD DEPOT
We were gluttonous and vile here in our Gomorrah! And now the Lord has seen fit to punish us!
Even the beasts of Hell pollute our skies as they did in centuries past!
SOUP

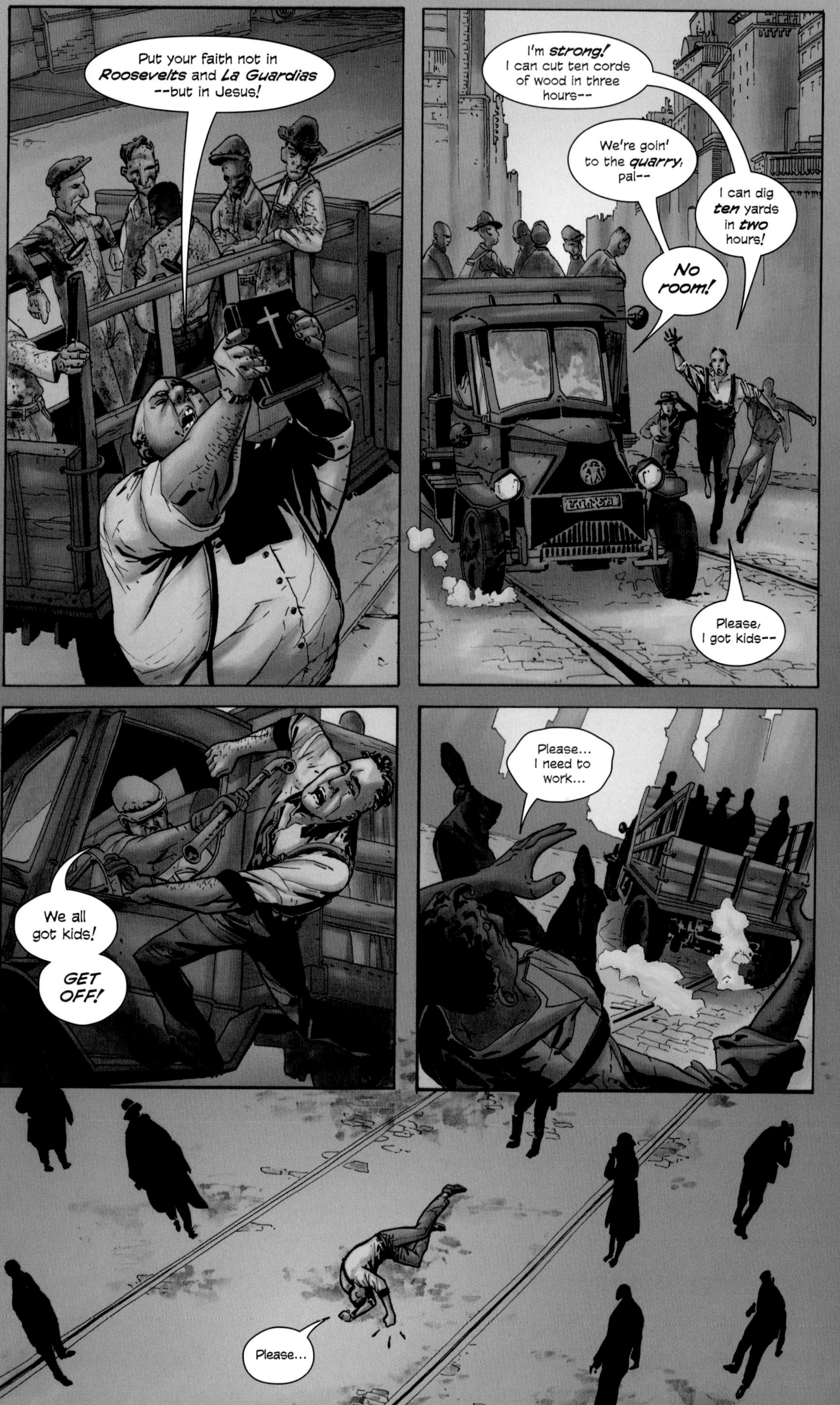

Put your faith not in *Roosevelts* and *La Guardias* --but in Jesus!
I'm ***strong!*** I can cut ten cords of wood in three hours--
We're goin' to the ***quarry,*** pal--
I can dig ***ten*** yards in ***two*** hours!
No room!
Please, I got kids--
We all got kids!
GET OFF!
Please... I need to work...
Please...

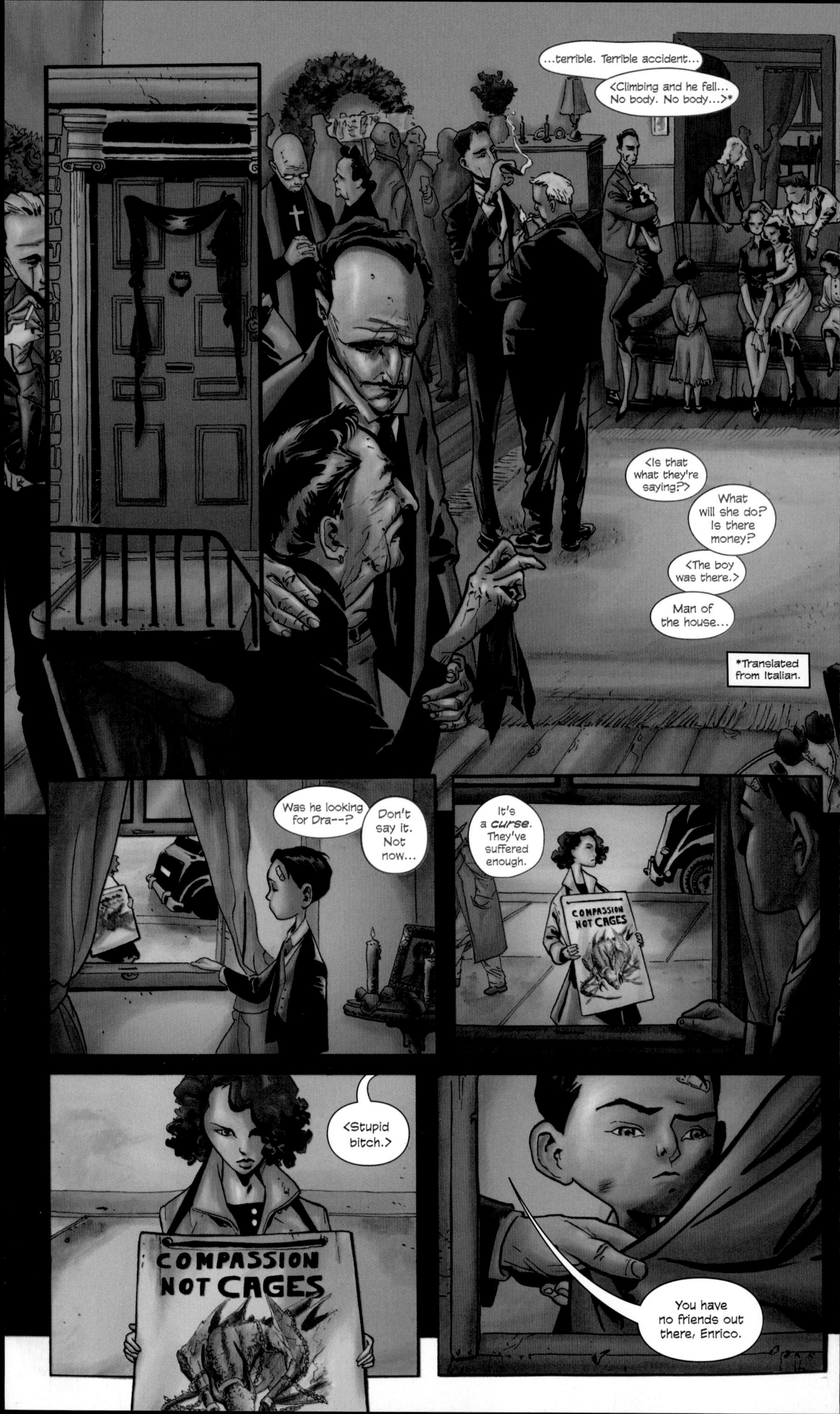

...terrible. Terrible accident...
<Climbing and he fell... No body. No body...>*
<Is that what they're saying?>
What will she do? Is there money?
<The boy was there.>
Man of the house...
*Translated from Italian.
Was he looking for Dra--?
Don't say it. Not now...
It's a *curse*. They've suffered enough.
COMPASSION NOT CAGES
<Stupid bitch.>
COMPASSION NOT CAGES
You have no friends out there, Enrico.

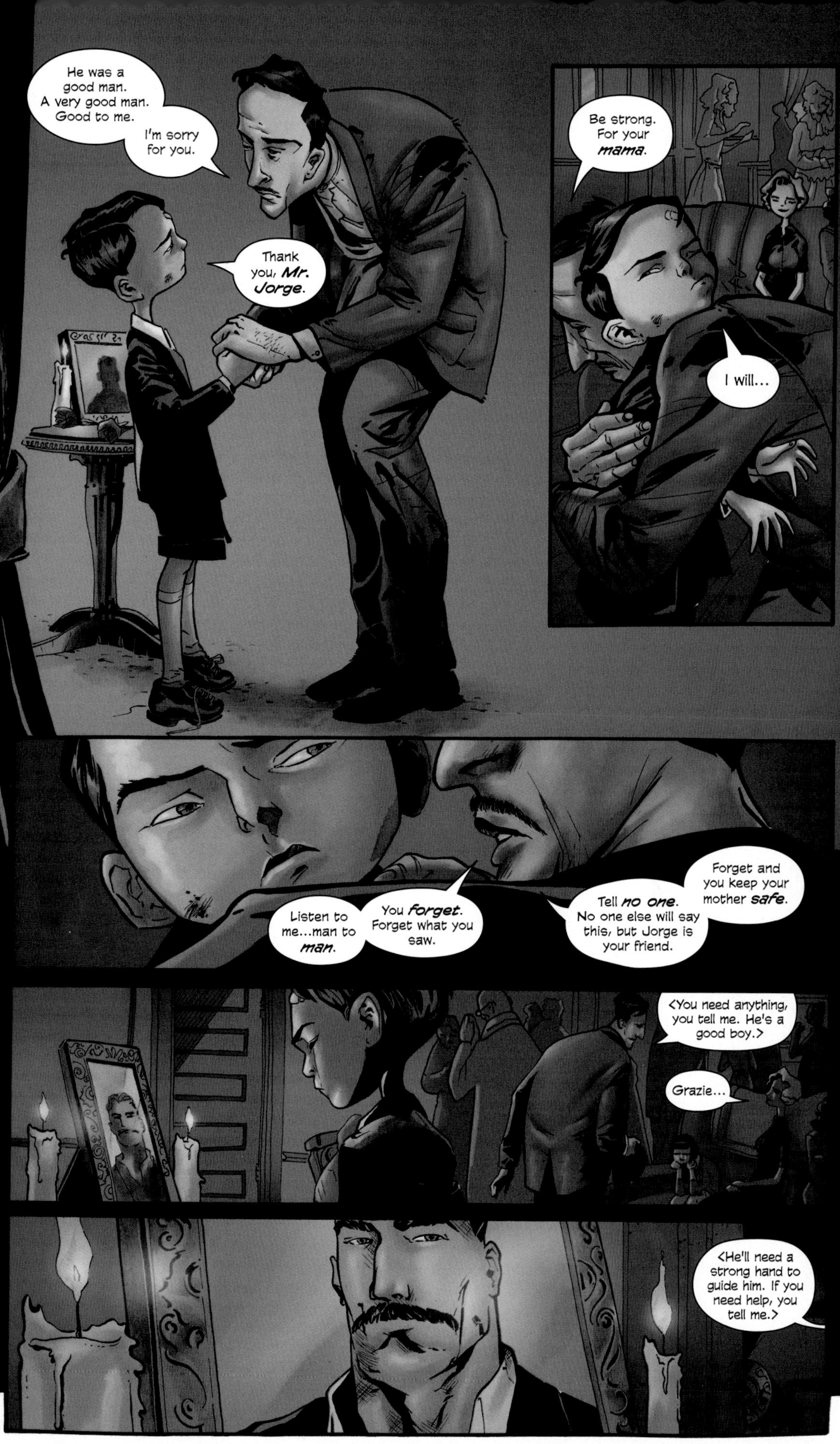
He was a good man. A very good man. Good to me.
I'm sorry for you.
Thank you, Mr. Jorge.
Be strong. For your mama.
I will...
Listen to me...man to man.
You forget. Forget what you saw.
Tell no one. No one else will say this, but Jorge is your friend.
Forget and you keep your mother safe.
<You need anything, you tell me. He's a good boy.>
Grazie...
<He'll need a strong hand to guide him. If you need help, you tell me.>

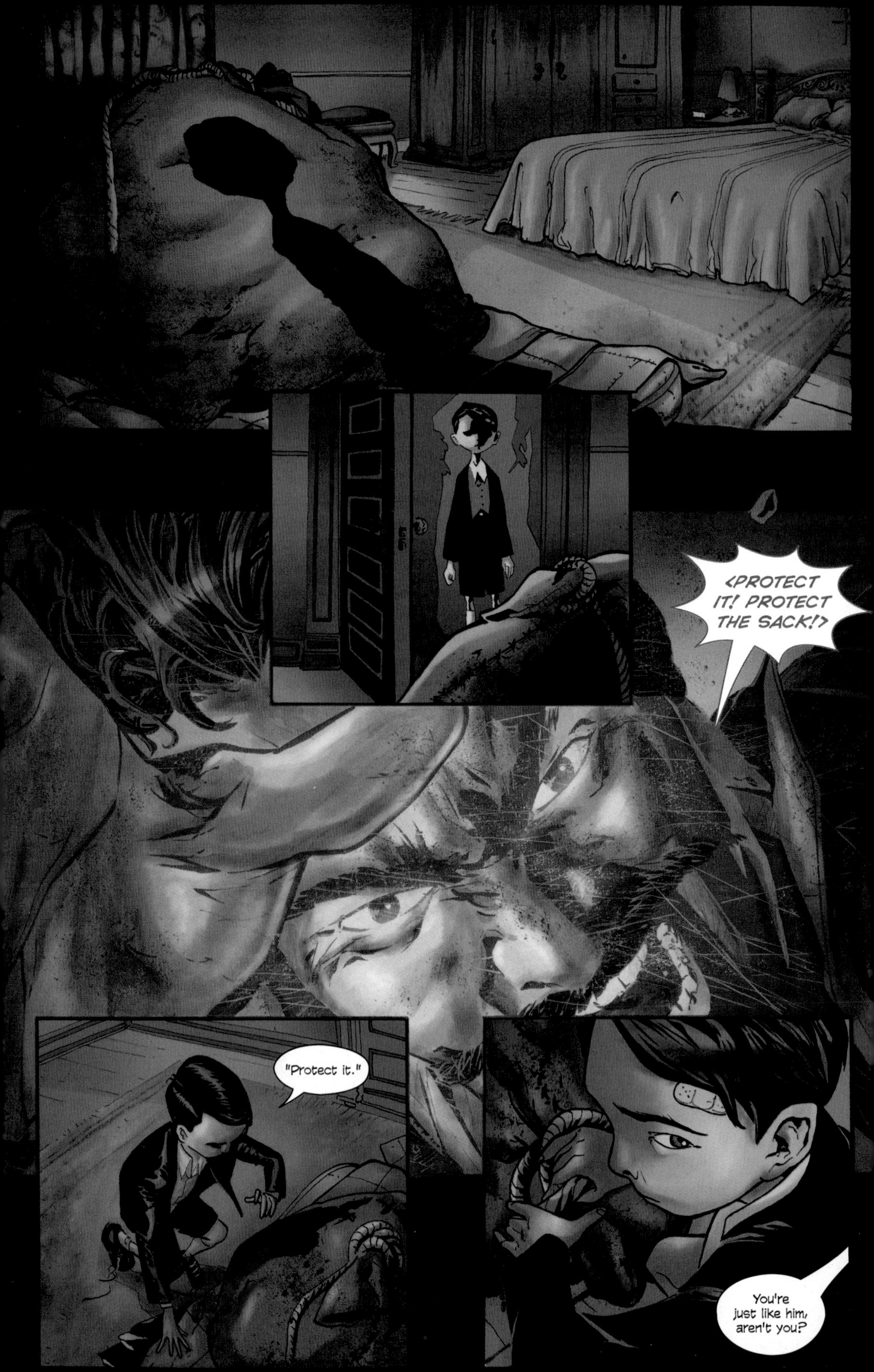
<PROTECT IT! PROTECT THE SACK!>
"Protect it."
You're just like him, aren't you?

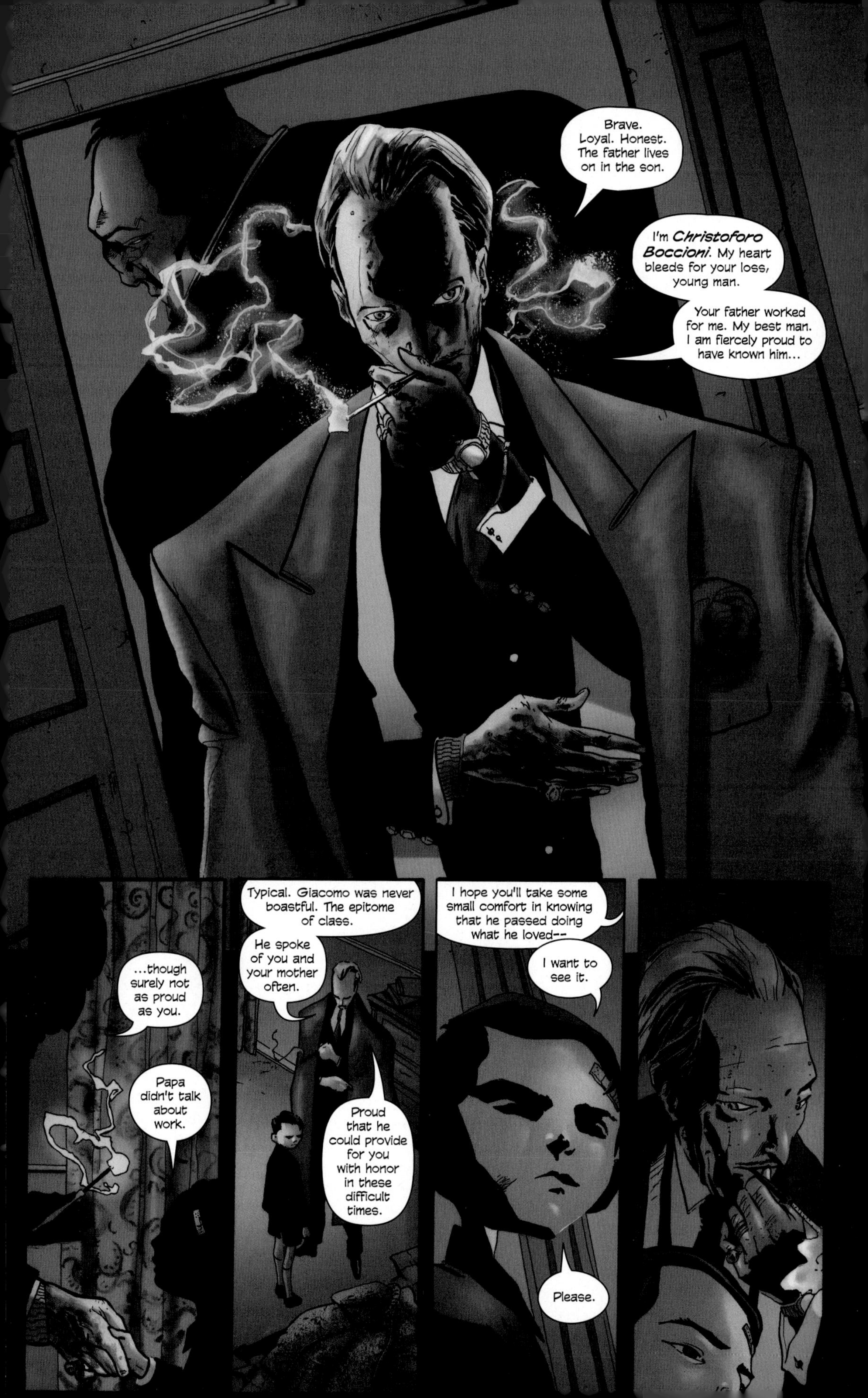
Brave. Loyal. Honest. The father lives on in the son.
I'm *Christoforo Boccioni*. My heart bleeds for your loss, young man.
Your father worked for me. My best man. I am fiercely proud to have known him...
...though surely not as proud as you.
Papa didn't talk about work.
Typical. Giacomo was never boastful. The epitome of class.
He spoke of you and your mother often.
Proud that he could provide for you with honor in these difficult times.
I hope you'll take some small comfort in knowing that he passed doing what he loved--
I want to see it.
Please.

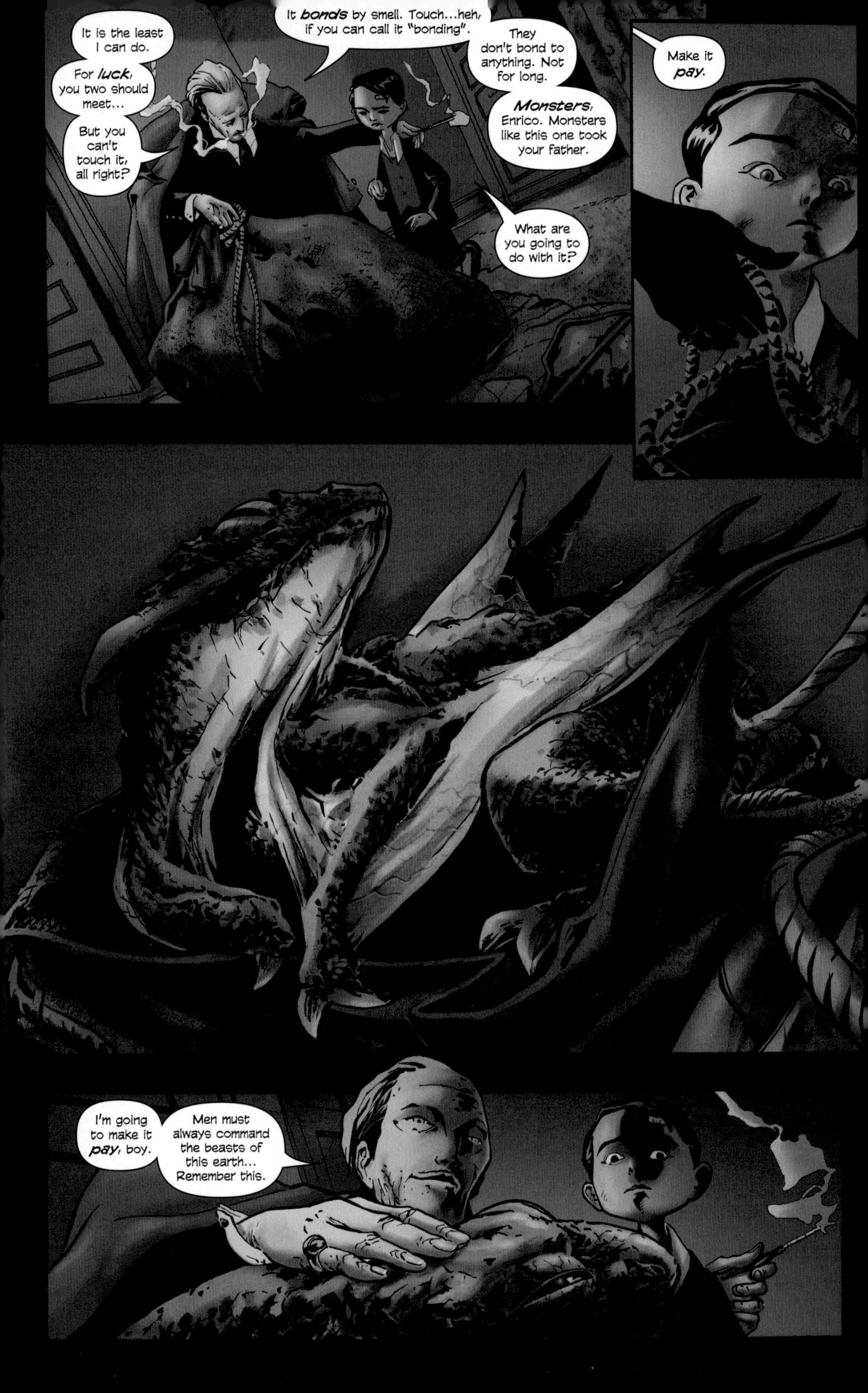
It is the least I can do.
For luck, you two should meet...
But you can't touch it, all right?
It bonds by smell. Touch...heh, if you can call it "bonding".
They don't bond to anything. Not for long.
Monsters, Enrico. Monsters like this one took your father.
What are you going to do with it?
Make it pay.
I'm going to make it pay, boy.
Men must always command the beasts of this earth... Remember this.

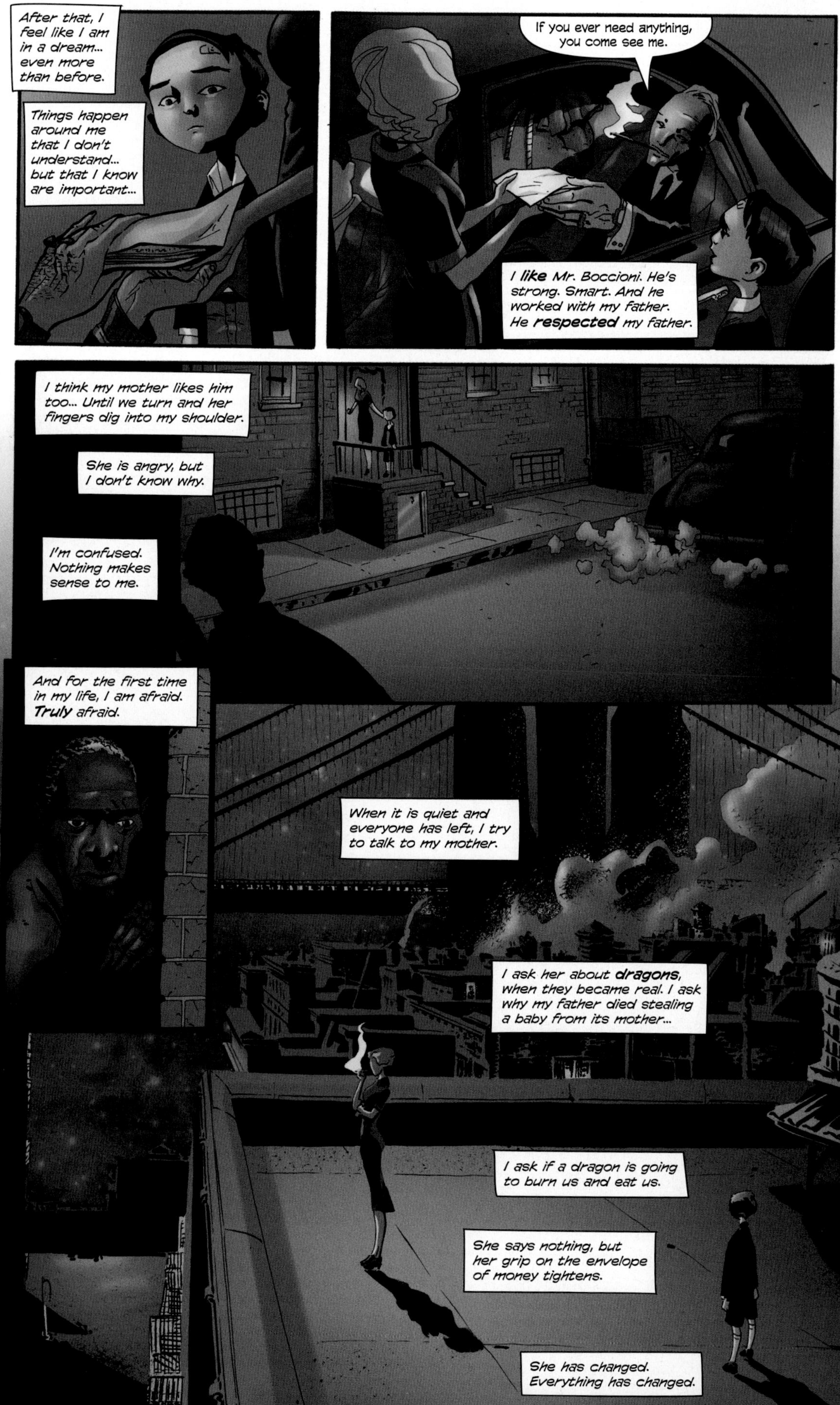
After that, I feel like I am in a dream... even more than before.
Things happen around me that I don't understand... but that I know are important...
If you ever need anything, you come see me.
I like Mr. Boccioni. He's strong. Smart. And he worked with my father. He respected my father.
I think my mother likes him too... Until we turn and her fingers dig into my shoulder.
She is angry, but I don't know why.
I'm confused. Nothing makes sense to me.
And for the first time in my life, I am afraid. Truly afraid.
When it is quiet and everyone has left, I try to talk to my mother.
I ask her about dragons, when they became real. I ask why my father died stealing a baby from its mother...
I ask if a dragon is going to burn us and eat us.
She says nothing, but her grip on the envelope of money tightens.
She has changed. Everything has changed.

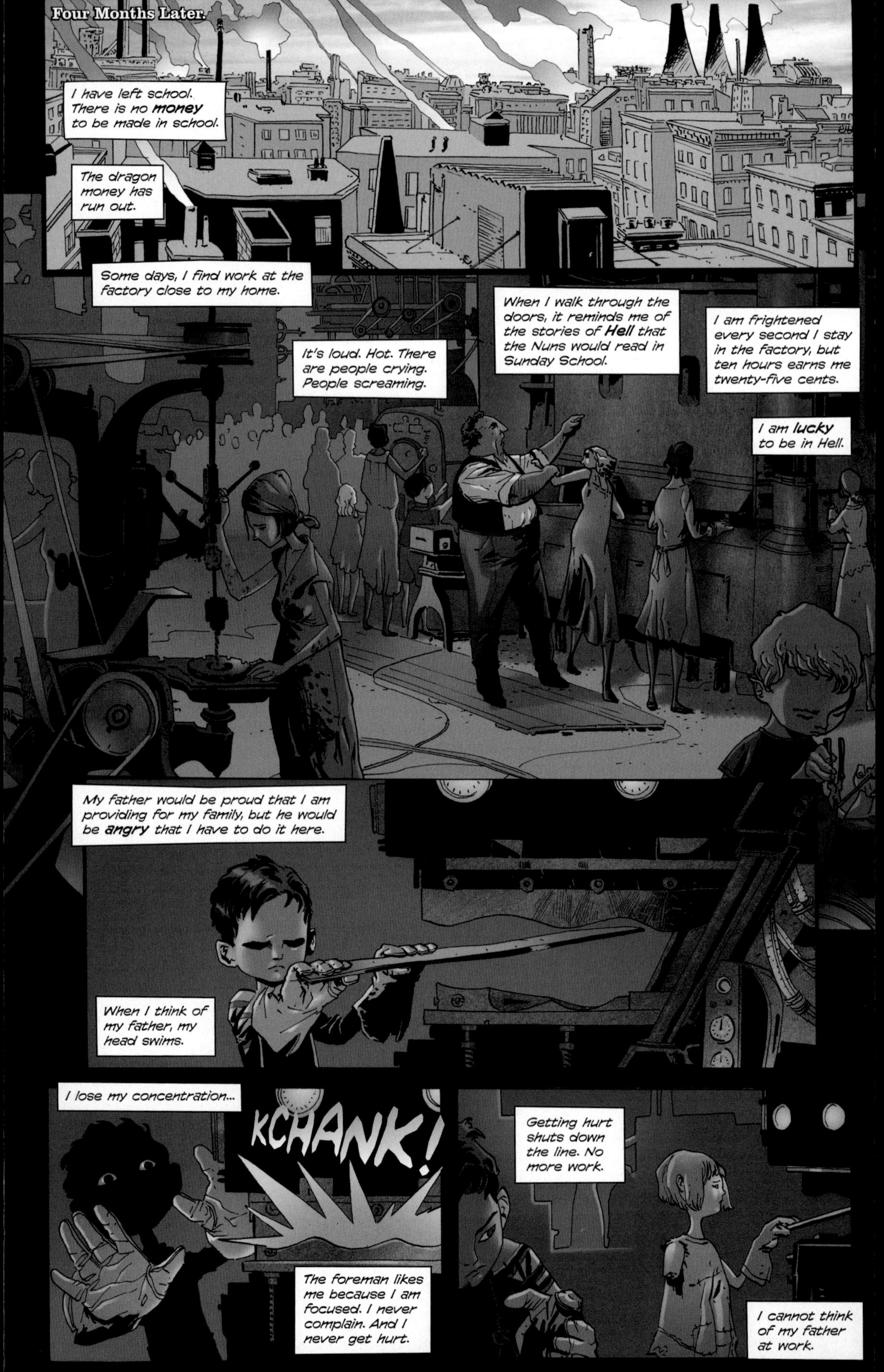

Four Months Later.
I have left school. There is no money to be made in school.
The dragon money has run out.
Some days, I find work at the factory close to my home.
It's loud. Hot. There are people crying. People screaming.
When I walk through the doors, it reminds me of the stories of Hell that the Nuns would read in Sunday School.
I am frightened every second I stay in the factory, but ten hours earns me twenty-five cents.
I am lucky to be in Hell.
My father would be proud that I am providing for my family, but he would be angry that I have to do it here.
When I think of my father, my head swims.
I lose my concentration...
KCHANK!
The foreman likes me because I am focused. I never complain. And I never get hurt.
Getting hurt shuts down the line. No more work.
I cannot think of my father at work.

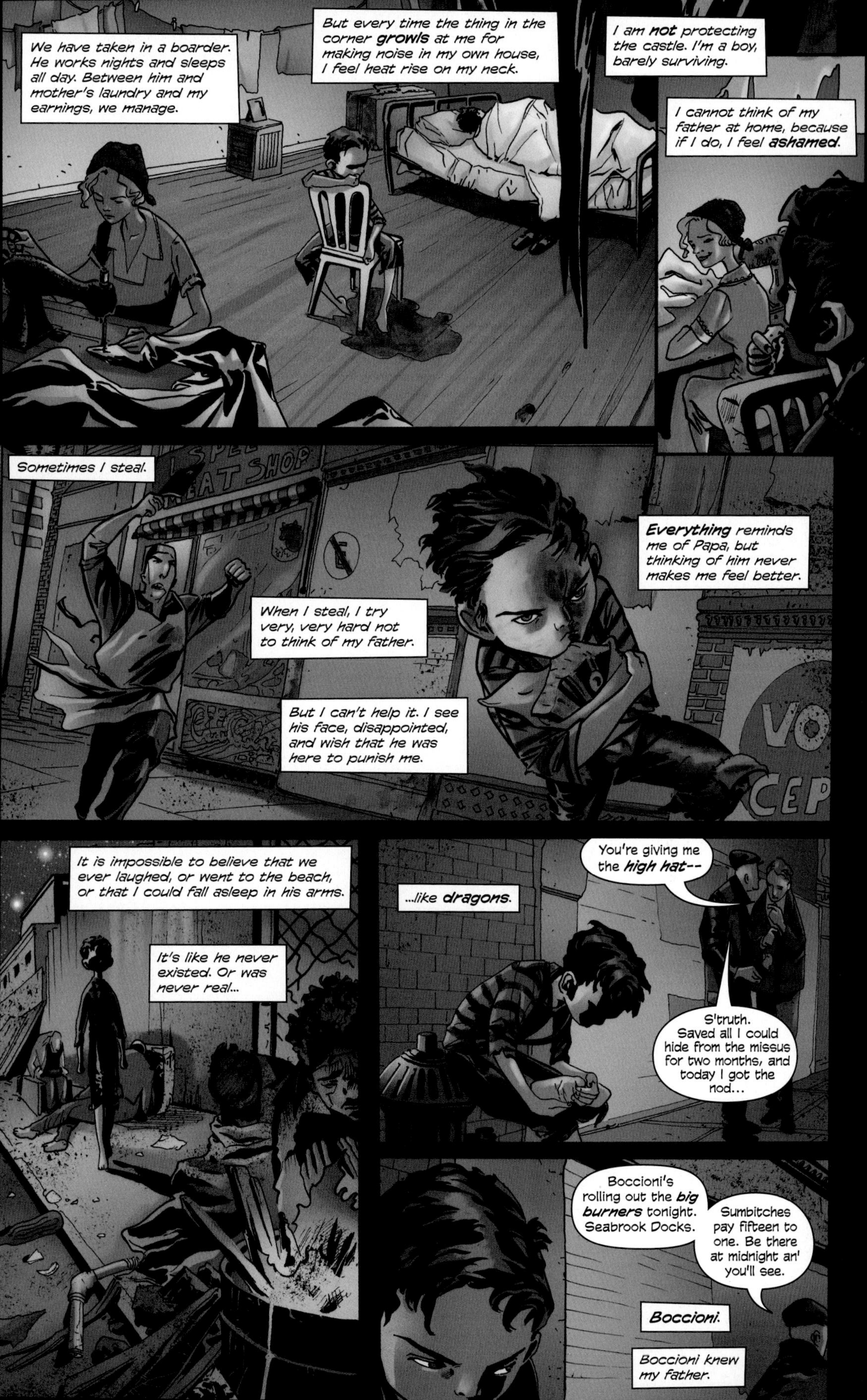
We have taken in a boarder. He works nights and sleeps all day. Between him and mother's laundry and my earnings, we manage.
But every time the thing in the corner growls at me for making noise in my own house, I feel heat rise on my neck.
I am not protecting the castle. I'm a boy, barely surviving.
I cannot think of my father at home, because if I do, I feel ashamed.
Sometimes I steal.
Everything reminds me of Papa, but thinking of him never makes me feel better.
When I steal, I try very, very hard not to think of my father.
But I can't help it. I see his face, disappointed, and wish that he was here to punish me.
It is impossible to believe that we ever laughed, or went to the beach, or that I could fall asleep in his arms.
It's like he never existed. Or was never real...
...like dragons.
You're giving me the high hat--
S'truth. Saved all I could hide from the missus for two months, and today I got the nod...
Boccioni's rolling out the big burners tonight. Seabrook Docks.
Sumbitches pay fifteen to one. Be there at midnight an' you'll see.
Boccioni.
Boccioni knew my father.

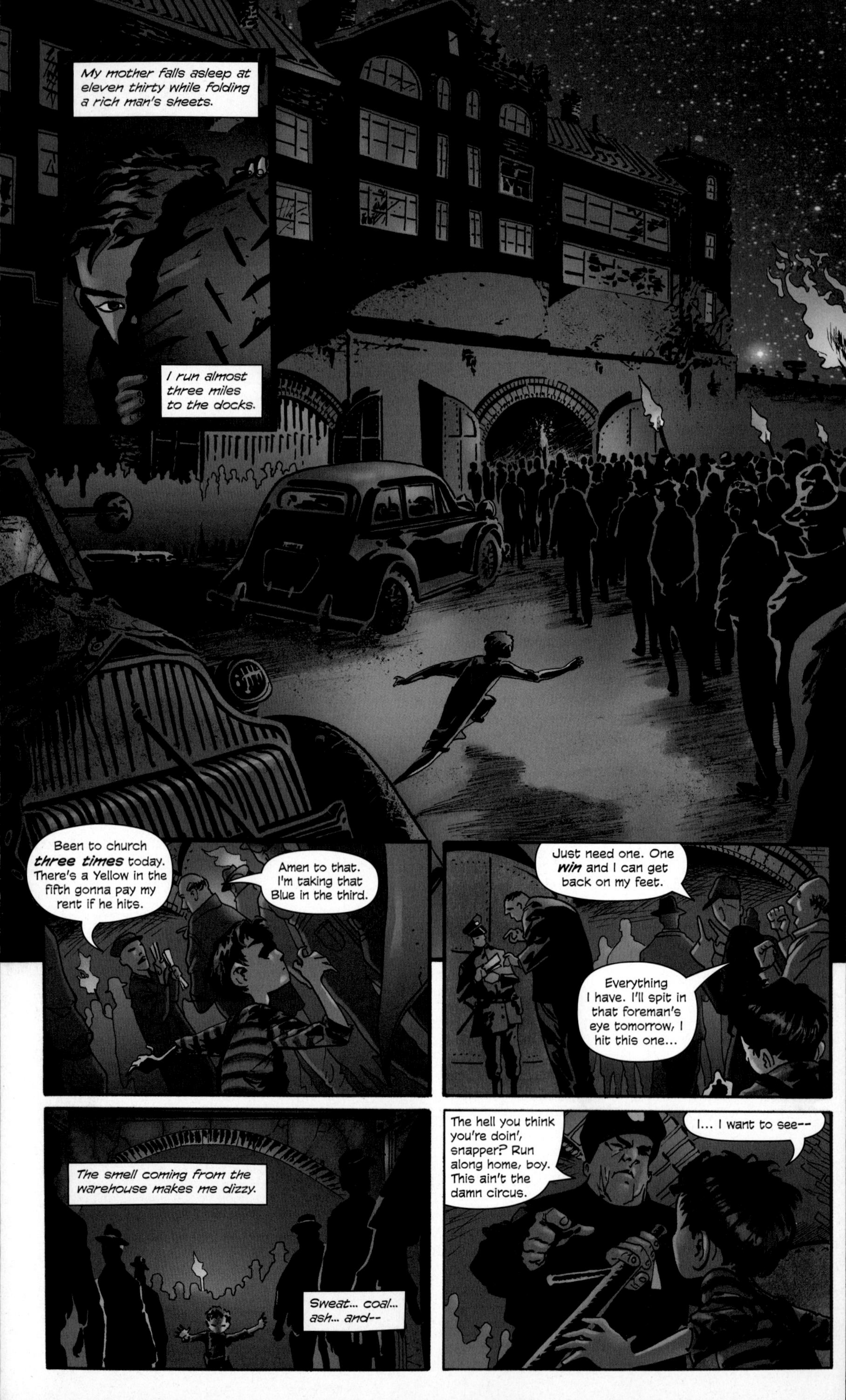
My mother falls asleep at eleven thirty while folding a rich man's sheets.
I run almost three miles to the docks.
Been to church three times today. There's a Yellow in the fifth gonna pay my rent if he hits.
Amen to that. I'm taking that Blue in the third.
Just need one. One win and I can get back on my feet.
Everything I have. I'll spit in that foreman's eye tomorrow, I hit this one...
The smell coming from the warehouse makes me dizzy.
Sweat... coal... ash... and--
The hell you think you're doin', snapper? Run along home, boy. This ain't the damn circus.
I... I want to see--

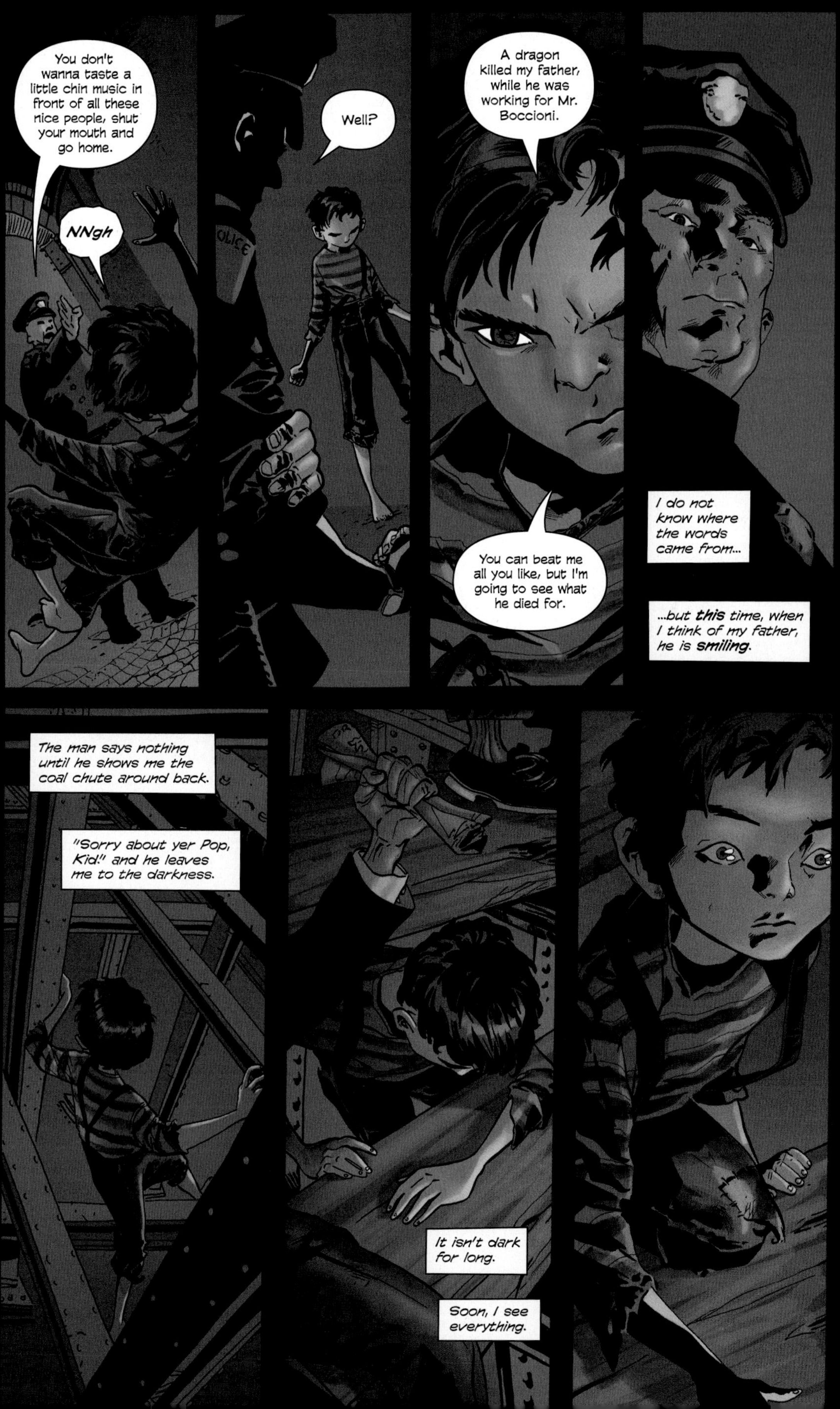
You don't wanna taste a little chin music in front of all these nice people, shut your mouth and go home.
NNgh
Well?
A dragon killed my father, while he was working for Mr. Boccioni.
You can beat me all you like, but I'm going to see what he died for.
I do not know where the words came from...
...but **this** time, when I think of my father, he is **smiling**.
The man says nothing until he shows me the coal chute around back.
"Sorry about yer Pop, Kid." and he leaves me to the darkness.
It isn't dark for long.
Soon, I see everything.

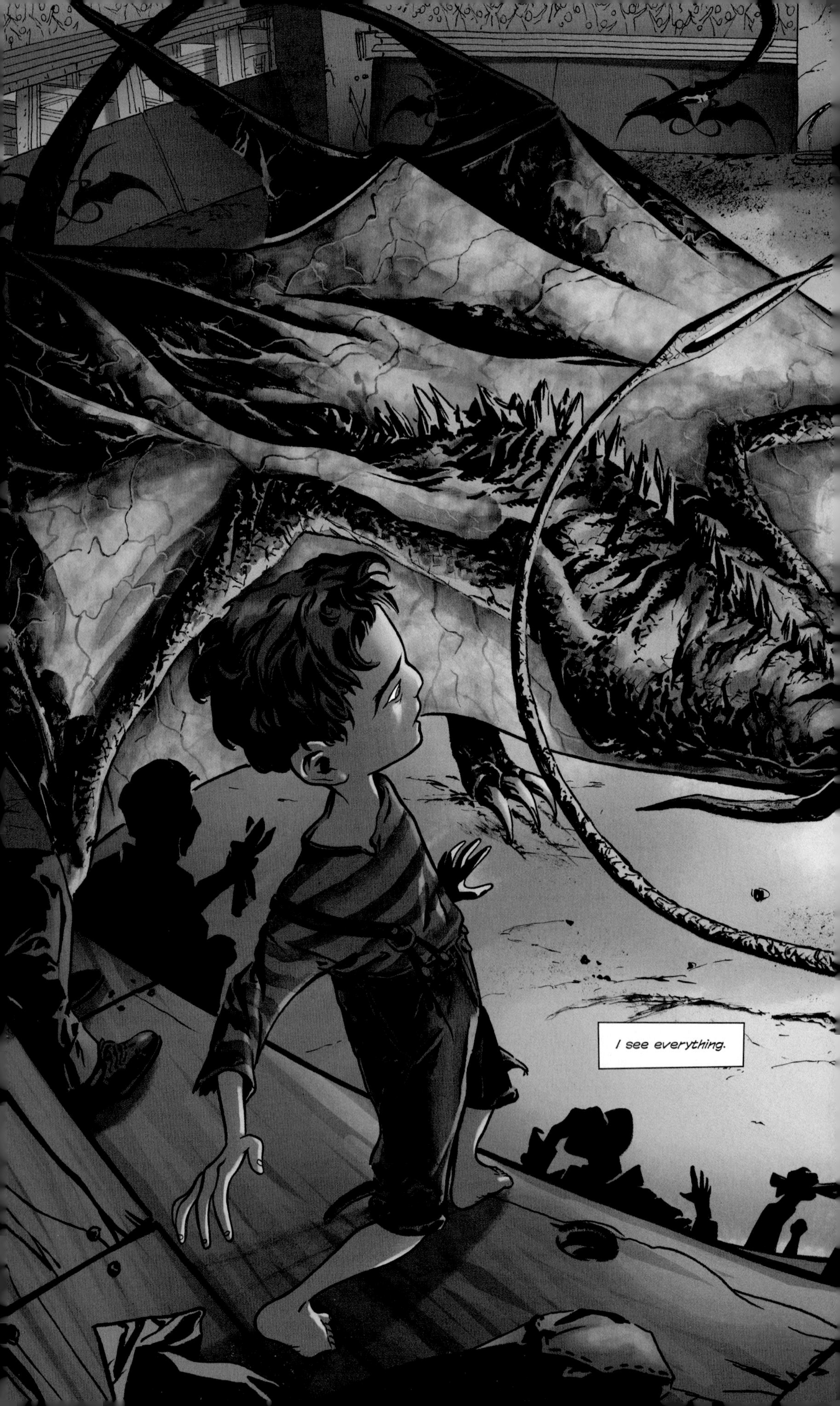
I see everything.

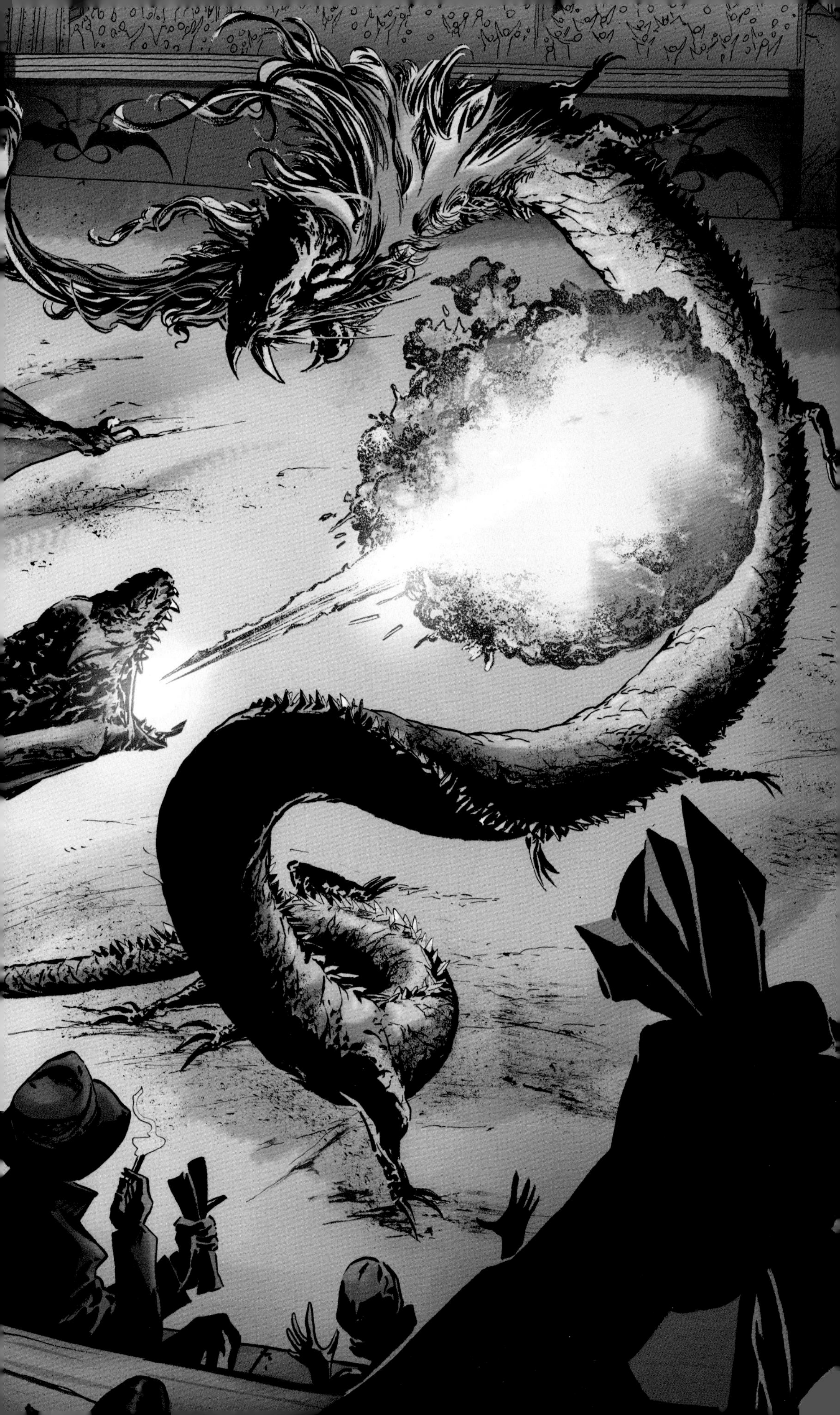

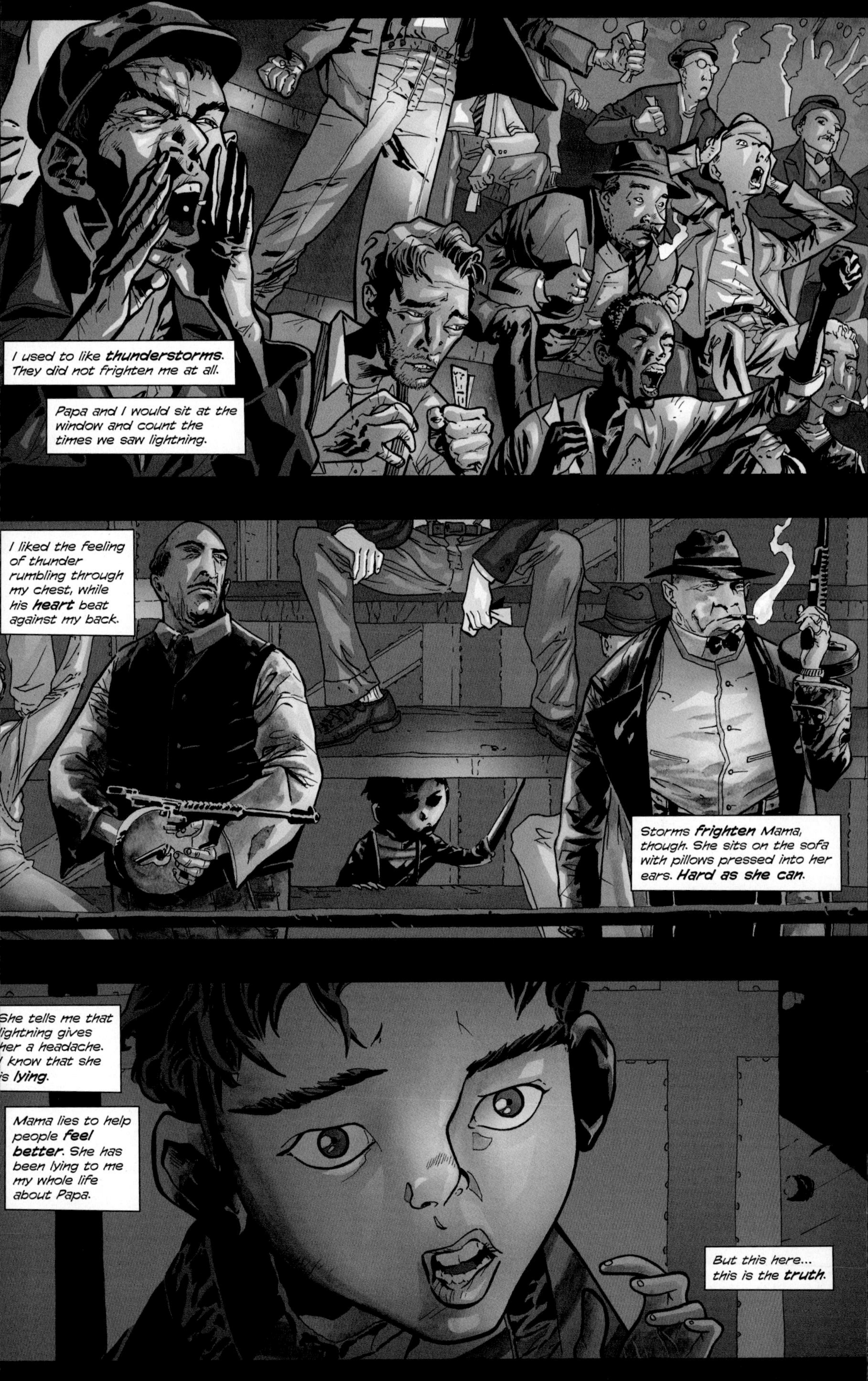
I used to like thunderstorms. They did not frighten me at all.
Papa and I would sit at the window and count the times we saw lightning.
I liked the feeling of thunder rumbling through my chest, while his heart beat against my back.
Storms frighten Mama, though. She sits on the sofa with pillows pressed into her ears. Hard as she can.
She tells me that lightning gives her a headache. I know that she is lying.
Mama lies to help people feel better. She has been lying to me my whole life about Papa.
But this here... this is the truth.

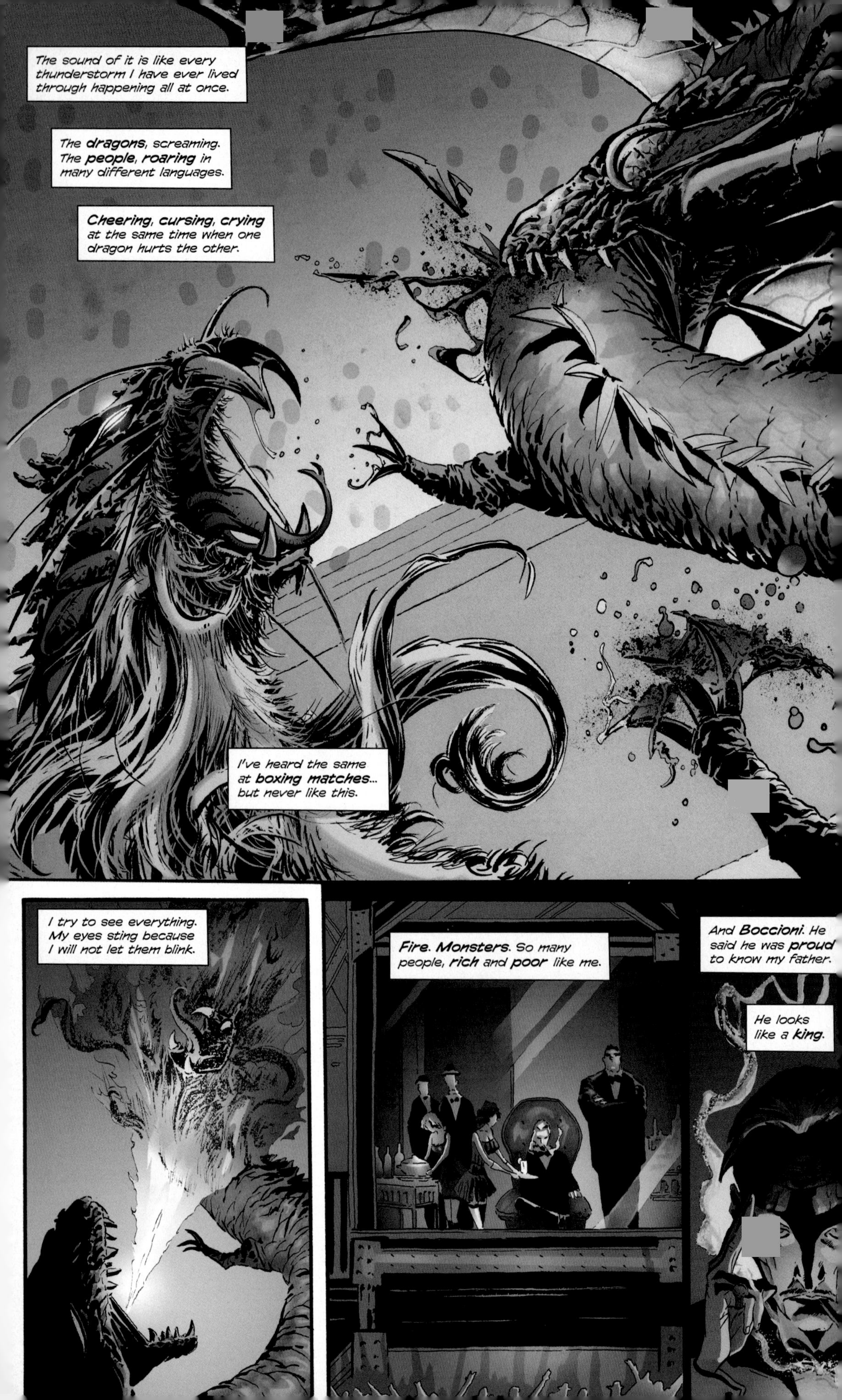
The sound of it is like every thunderstorm I have ever lived through happening all at once.
The dragons, screaming. The people, roaring in many different languages.
Cheering, cursing, crying at the same time when one dragon hurts the other.
I've heard the same at boxing matches... but never like this.
I try to see everything. My eyes sting because I will not let them blink.
Fire. Monsters. So many people, rich and poor like me.
And Boccioni. He said he was proud to know my father.
He looks like a king.

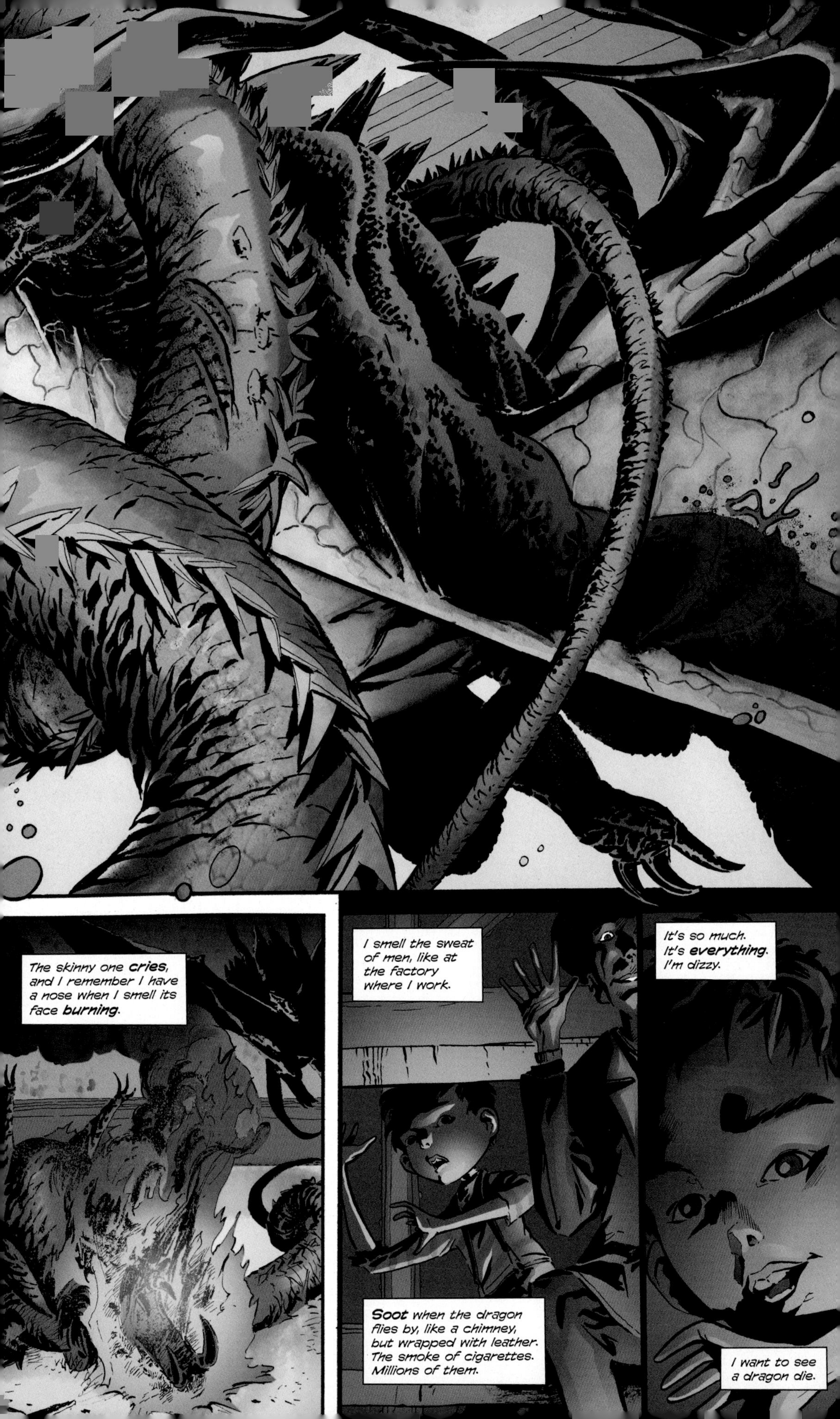
The skinny one **cries**, and I remember I have a nose when I smell its face **burning**.
I smell the sweat of men, like at the factory where I work.
Soot when the dragon flies by, like a chimney, but wrapped with leather. The smoke of cigarettes. Millions of them.
It's so much. It's **everything**. I'm dizzy.
I want to see a dragon die.

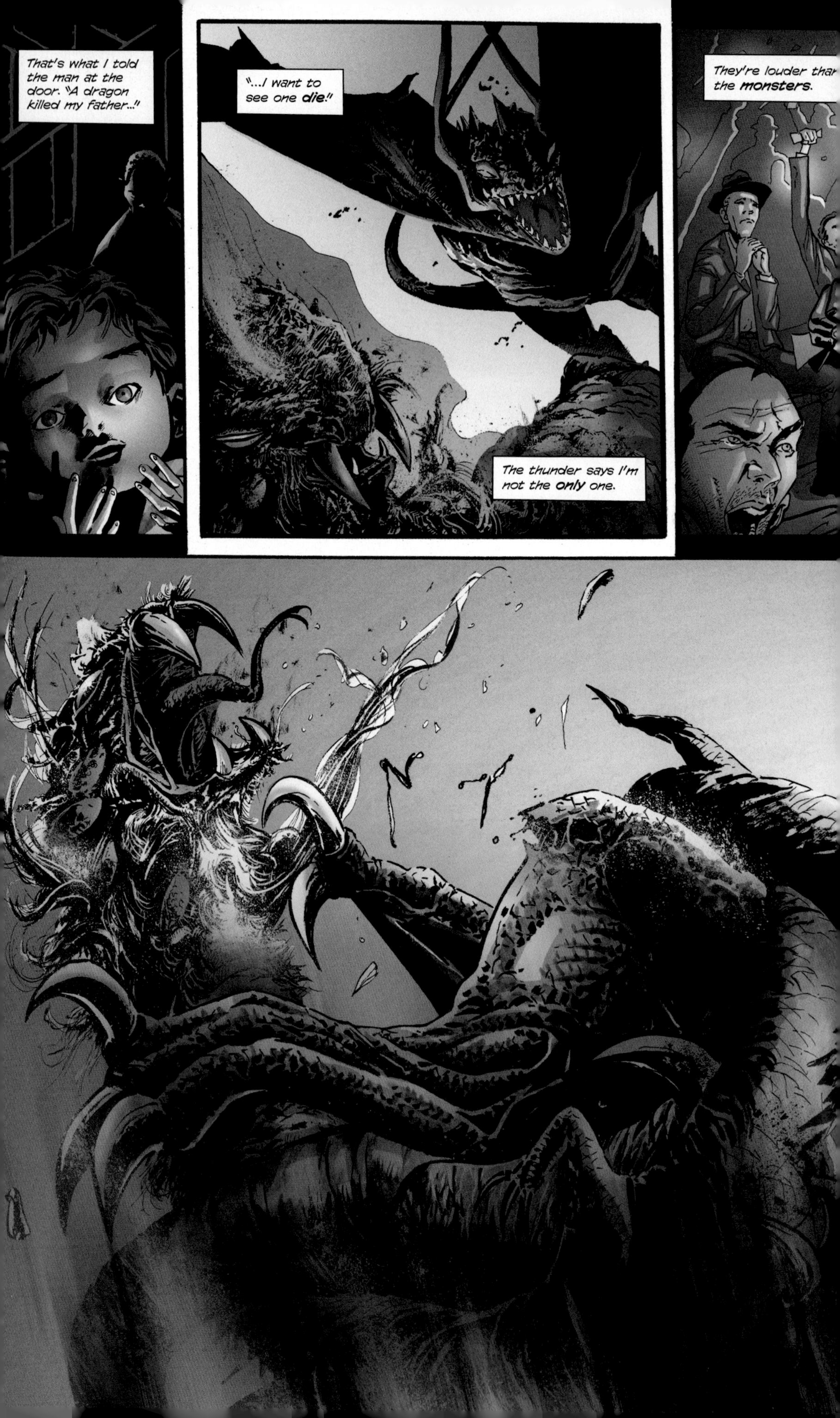
That's what I told the man at the door. "A dragon killed my father..."
"...I want to see one die."
The thunder says I'm not the only one.
They're louder than the monsters.

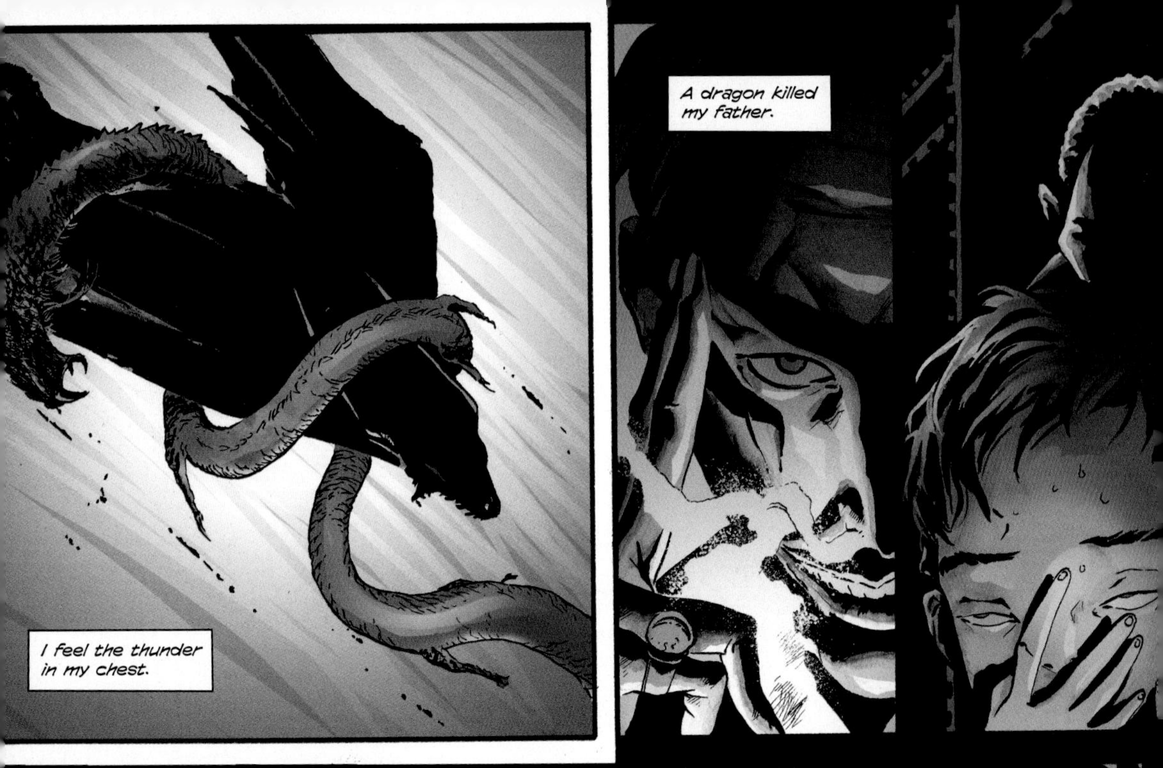
I feel the thunder in my chest.
A dragon killed my father.

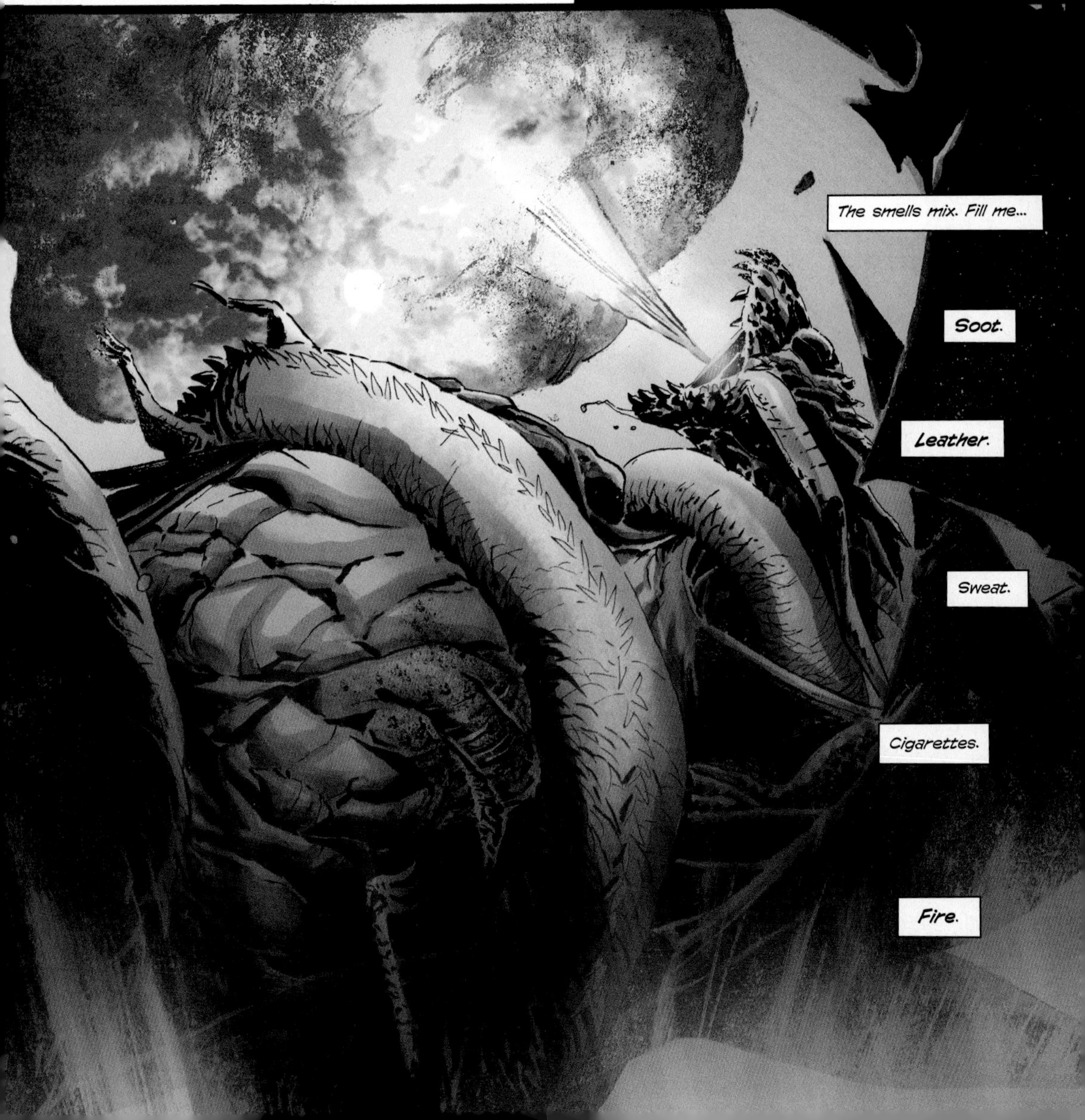
The smells mix. Fill me...
Soot.
Leather.
Sweat.
Cigarettes.
Fire.

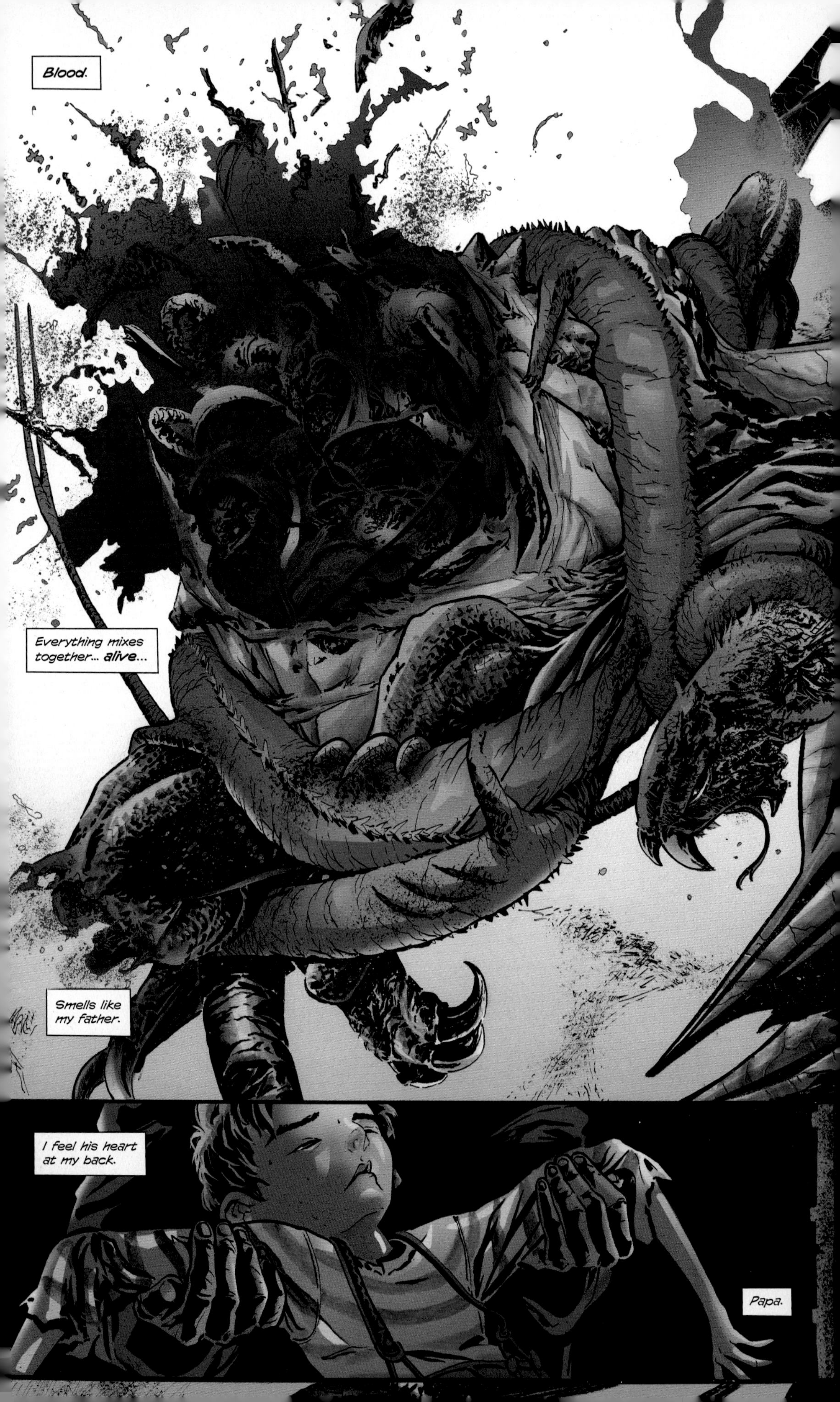
Blood.
Everything mixes together... alive...
Smells like my father.
I feel his heart at my back.
Papa.

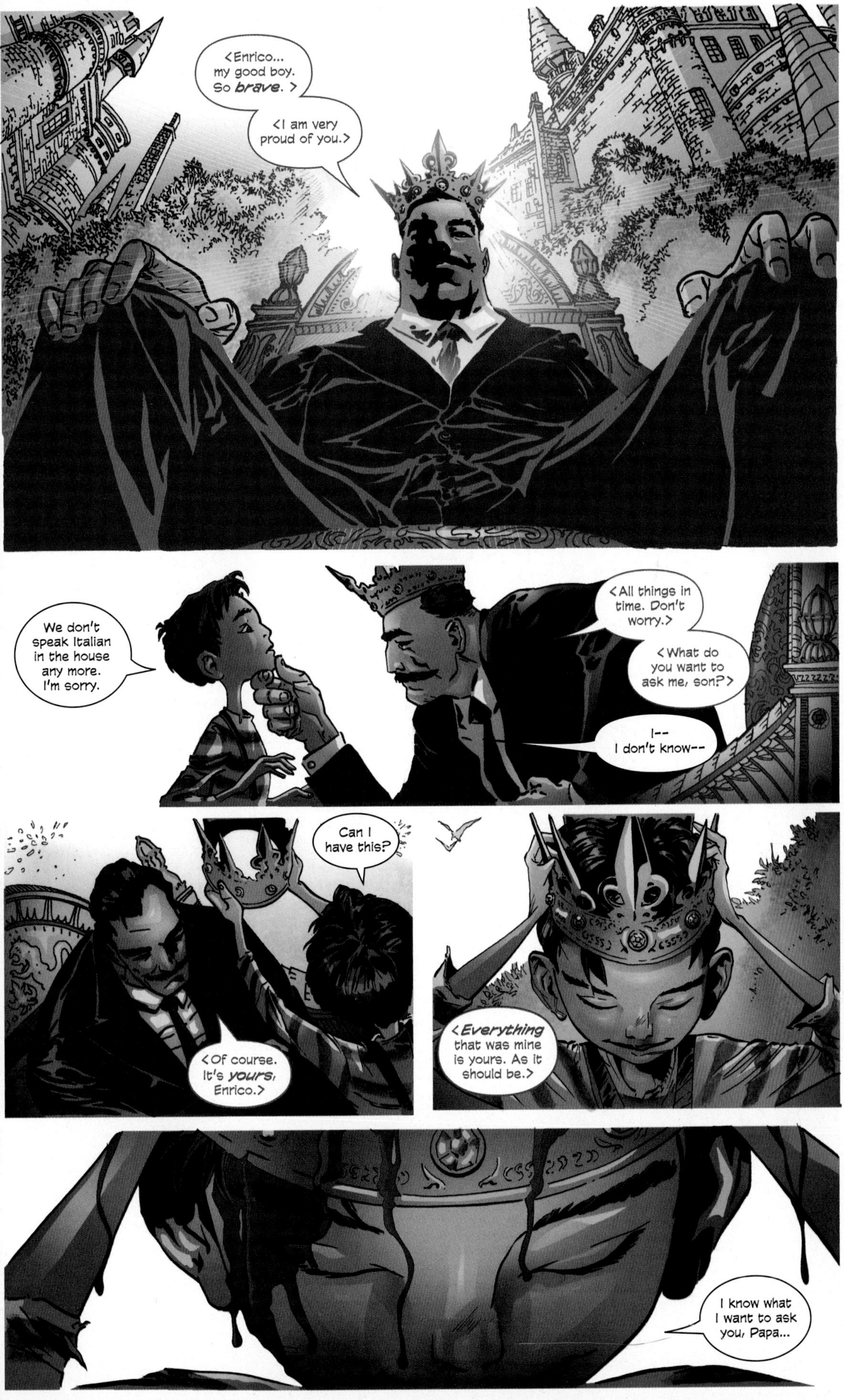
<Enrico... my good boy. So brave.>
<I am very proud of you.>
We don't speak Italian in the house any more. I'm sorry.
<All things in time. Don't worry.>
<What do you want to ask me, son?>
I-- I don't know--
Can I have this?
<Of course. It's yours, Enrico.>
<Everything that was mine is yours. As it should be.>
I know what I want to ask you, Papa...

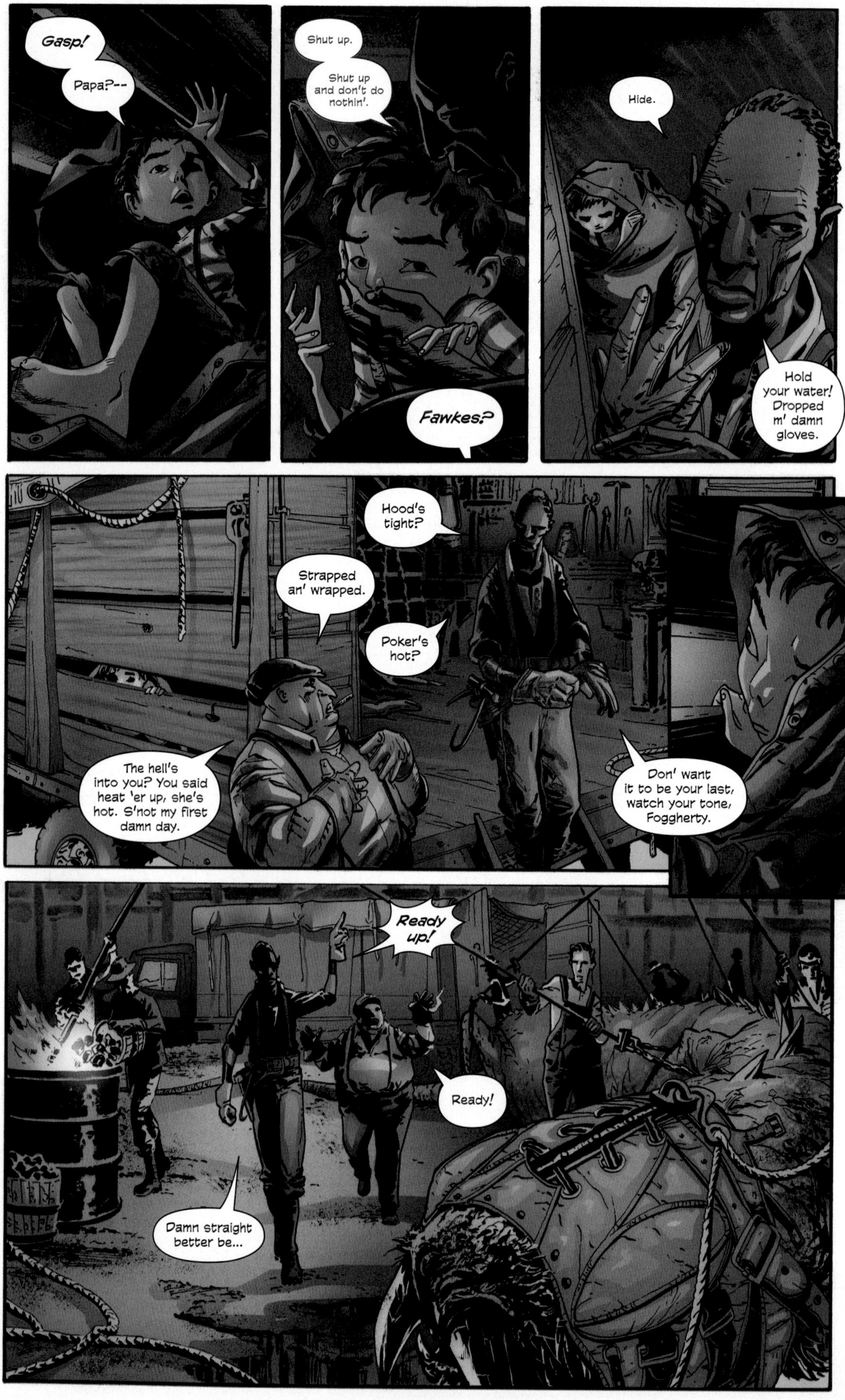
Gasp!
Papa?--
Shut up.
Shut up and don't do nothin'.
Fawkes?
Hide.
Hold your water! Dropped m' damn gloves.
Hood's tight?
Strapped an' wrapped.
Poker's hot?
The hell's into you? You said heat 'er up, she's hot. S'not my first damn day.
Don' want it to be your last, watch your tone, Foggherty.
Ready up!
Ready!
Damn straight better be...

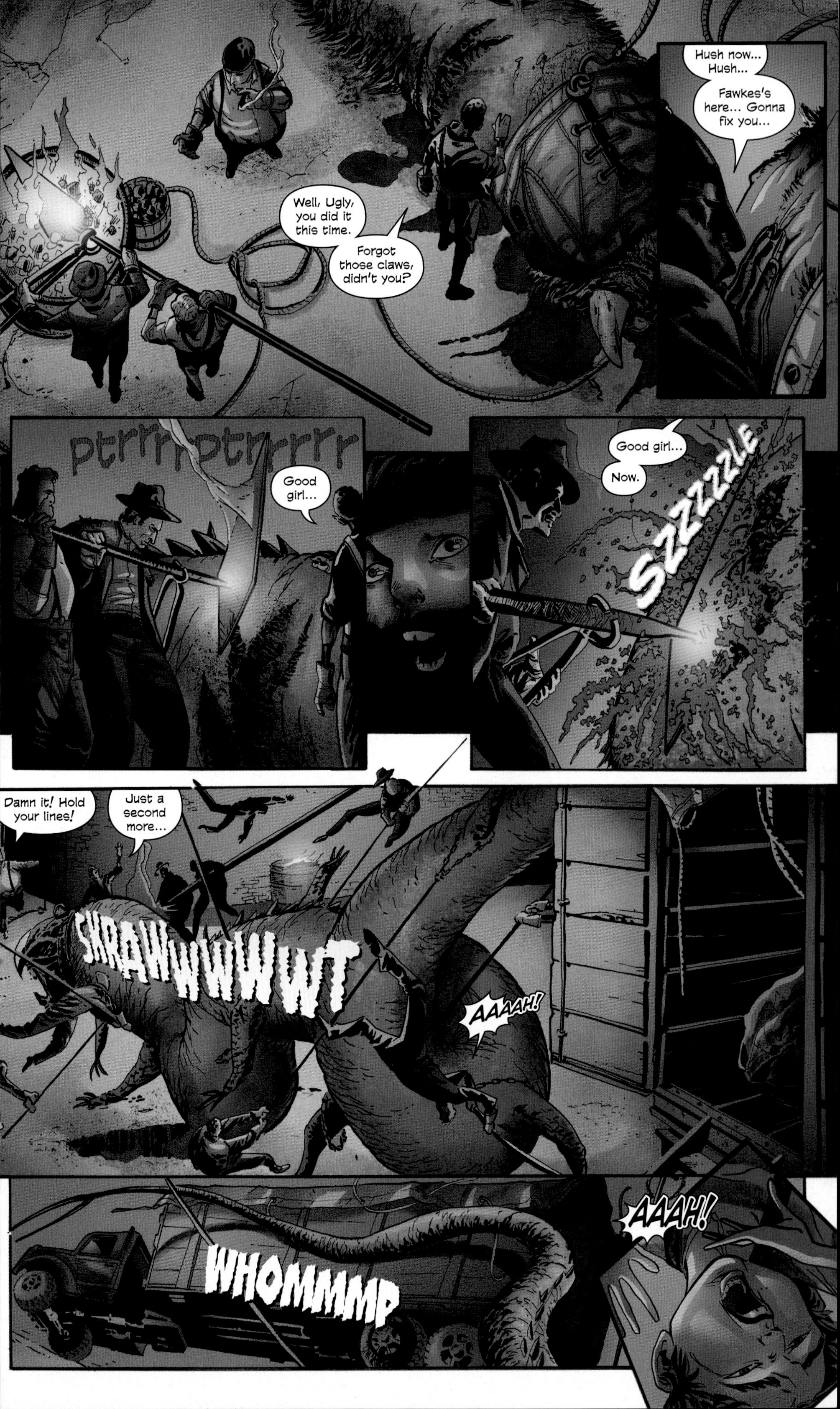
Well, Ugly, you did it this time.
Forgot those claws, didn't you?
Hush now... Hush...
Fawkes's here... Gonna fix you...
ptrrrrptrrrrrr
Good girl...
Good girl...
Now.
SZZZZZZLE
Damn it! Hold your lines!
Just a second more...
SHRAWWWWWT
AAAAH!
AAAH!
WHOMMMMP

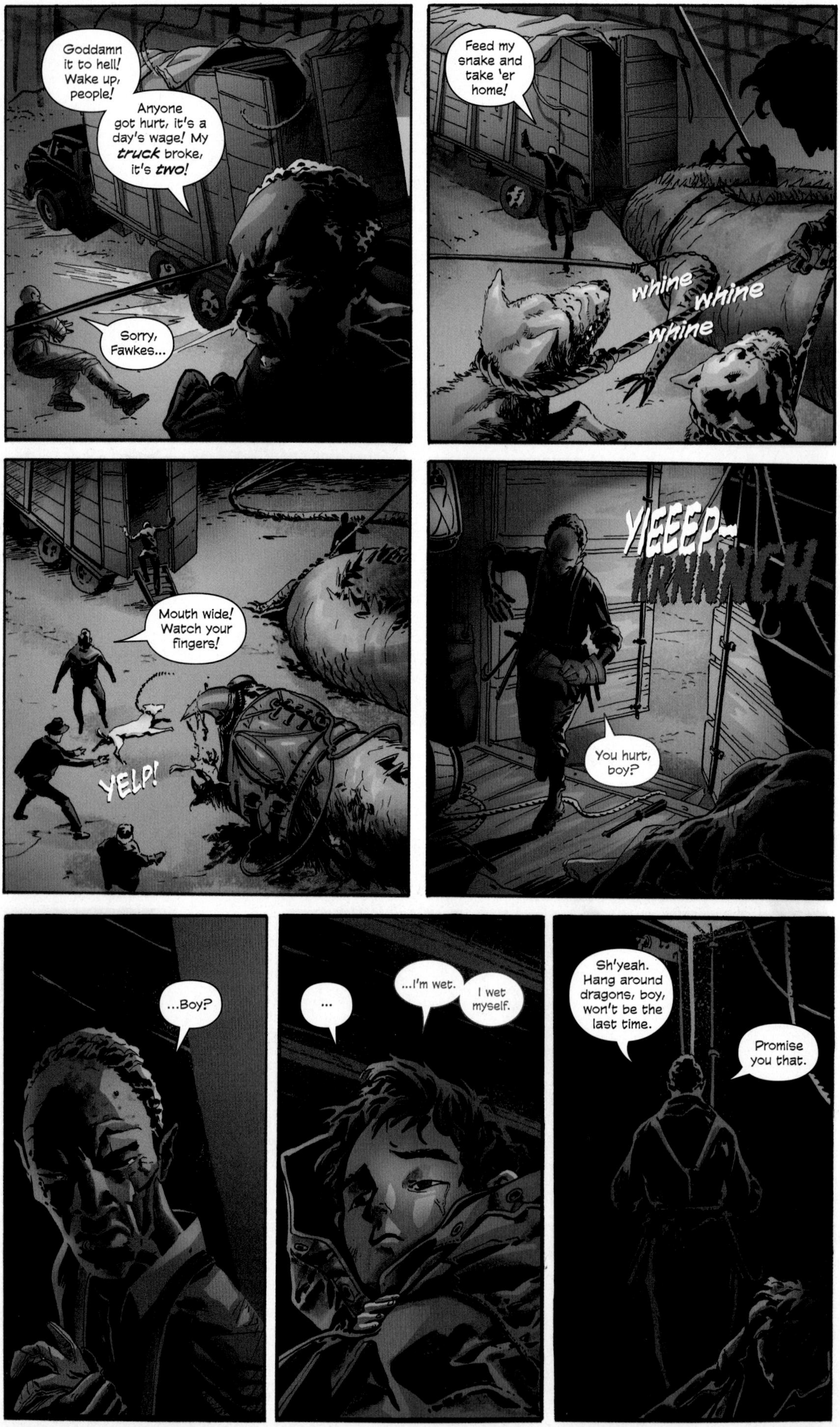
Goddamn it to hell! Wake up, people!
Anyone got hurt, it's a day's wage! My truck broke, it's two!
Sorry, Fawkes...
Feed my snake and take 'er home!
whine
whine
whine
Mouth wide! Watch your fingers!
YELP!
YIEEEP—
KRNNNCH
You hurt, boy?
...Boy?
...
...I'm wet.
I wet myself.
Sh'yeah. Hang around dragons, boy, won't be the last time.
Promise you that.

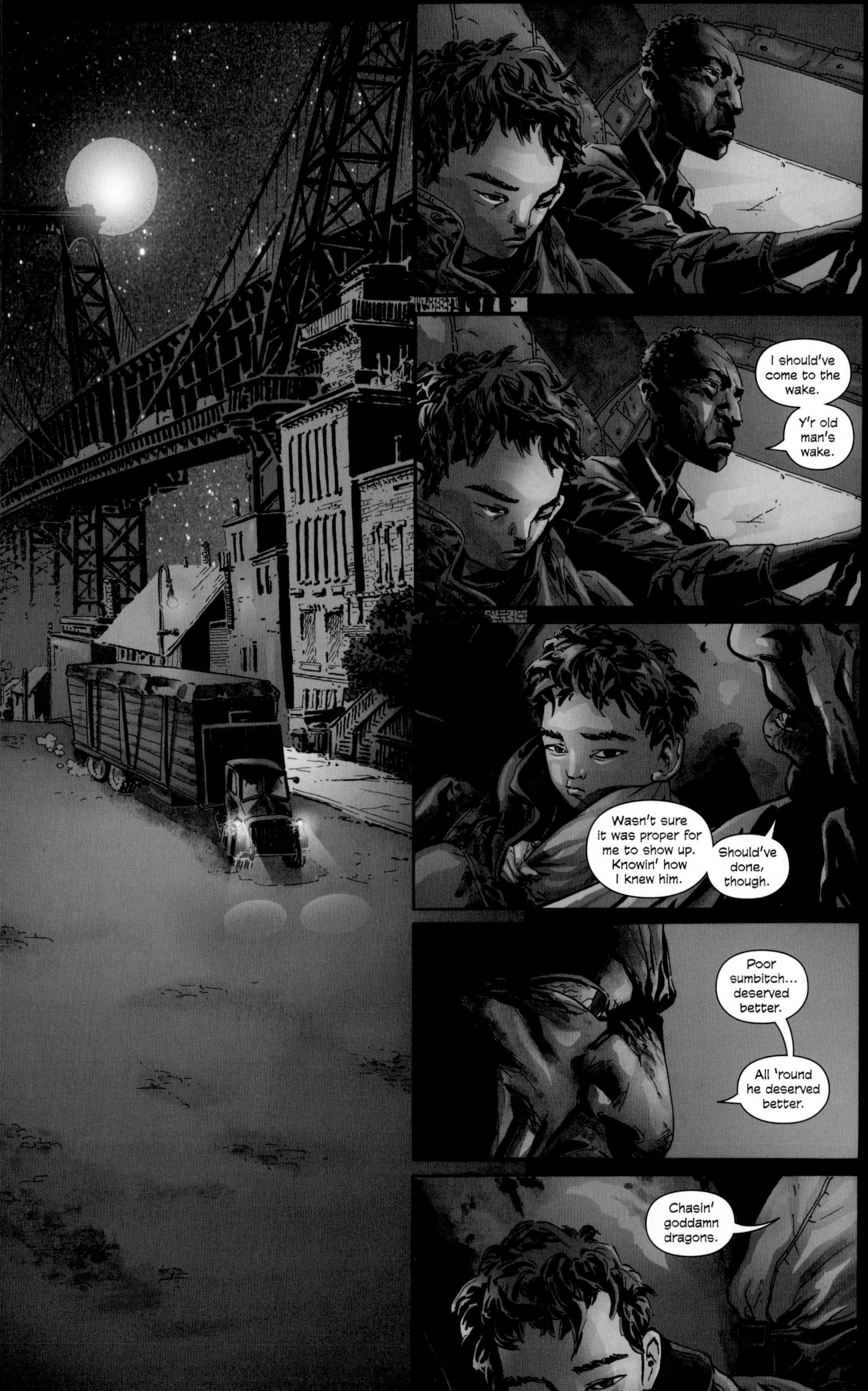
I should've come to the wake.
Y'r old man's wake.
Wasn't sure it was proper for me to show up. Knowin' how I knew him.
Should've done, though.
Poor sumbitch... deserved better.
All 'round he deserved better.
Chasin' goddamn dragons.

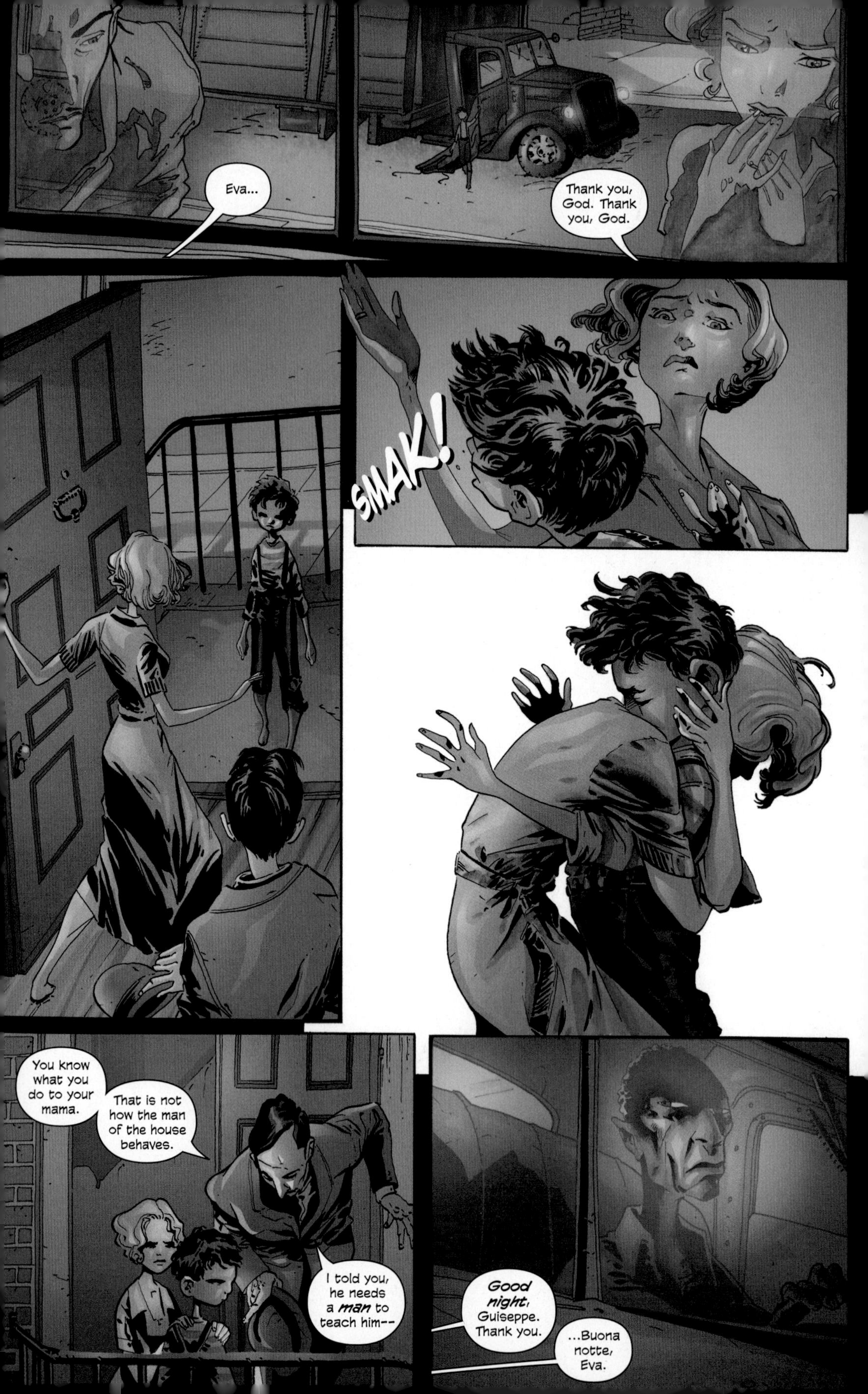
Eva...
Thank you, God. Thank you, God.
SMAK!
You know what you do to your mama.
That is not how the man of the house behaves.
I told you, he needs a *man* to teach him--
Good night, Guiseppe. Thank you.
...Buona notte, Eva.

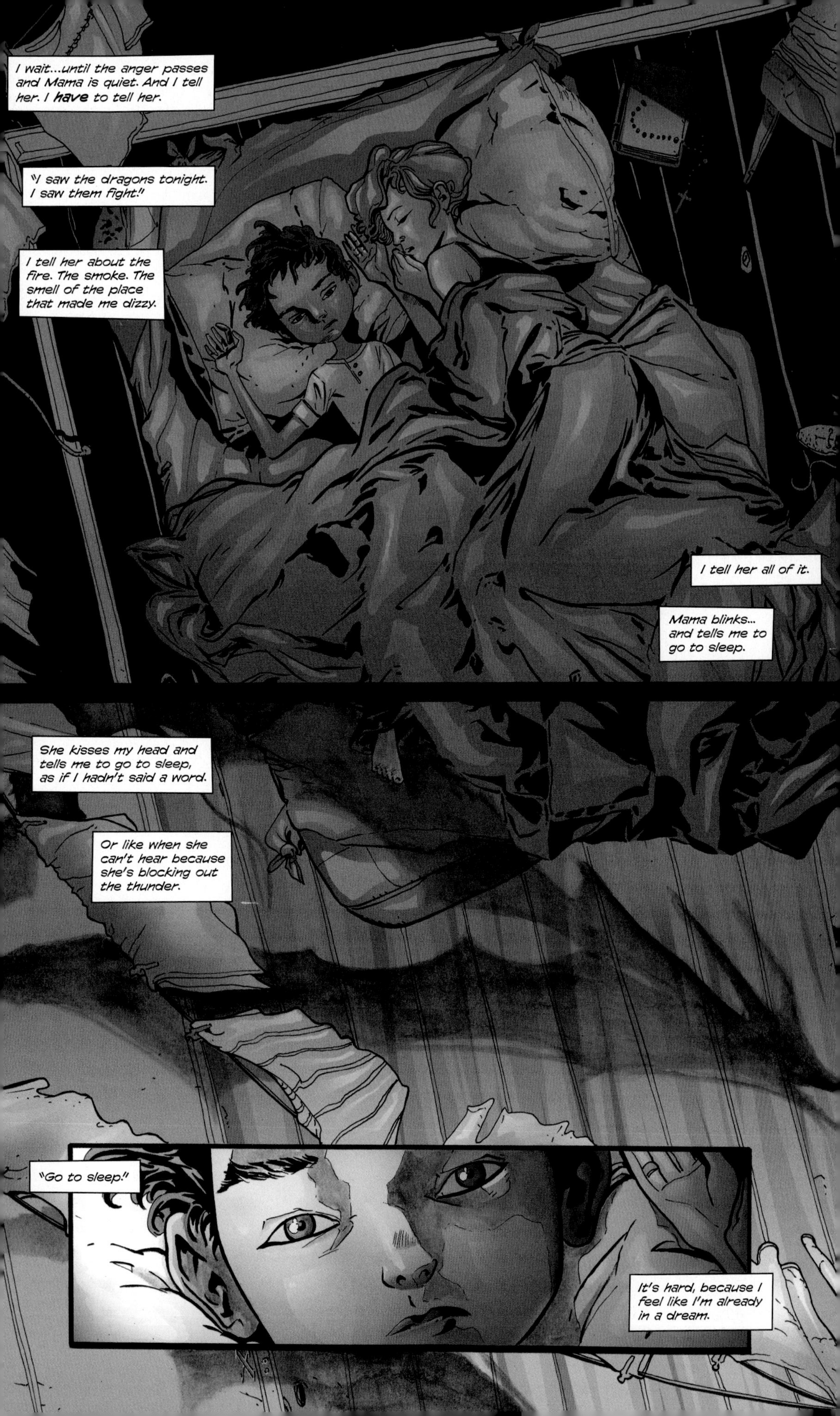
I wait...until the anger passes and Mama is quiet. And I tell her. I **have** to tell her.
"I saw the dragons tonight. I saw them fight."
I tell her about the fire. The smoke. The smell of the place that made me dizzy.
I tell her all of it.
Mama blinks... and tells me to go to sleep.
She kisses my head and tells me to go to sleep, as if I hadn't said a word.
Or like when she can't hear because she's blocking out the thunder.
"Go to sleep."
It's hard, because I feel like I'm already in a dream.

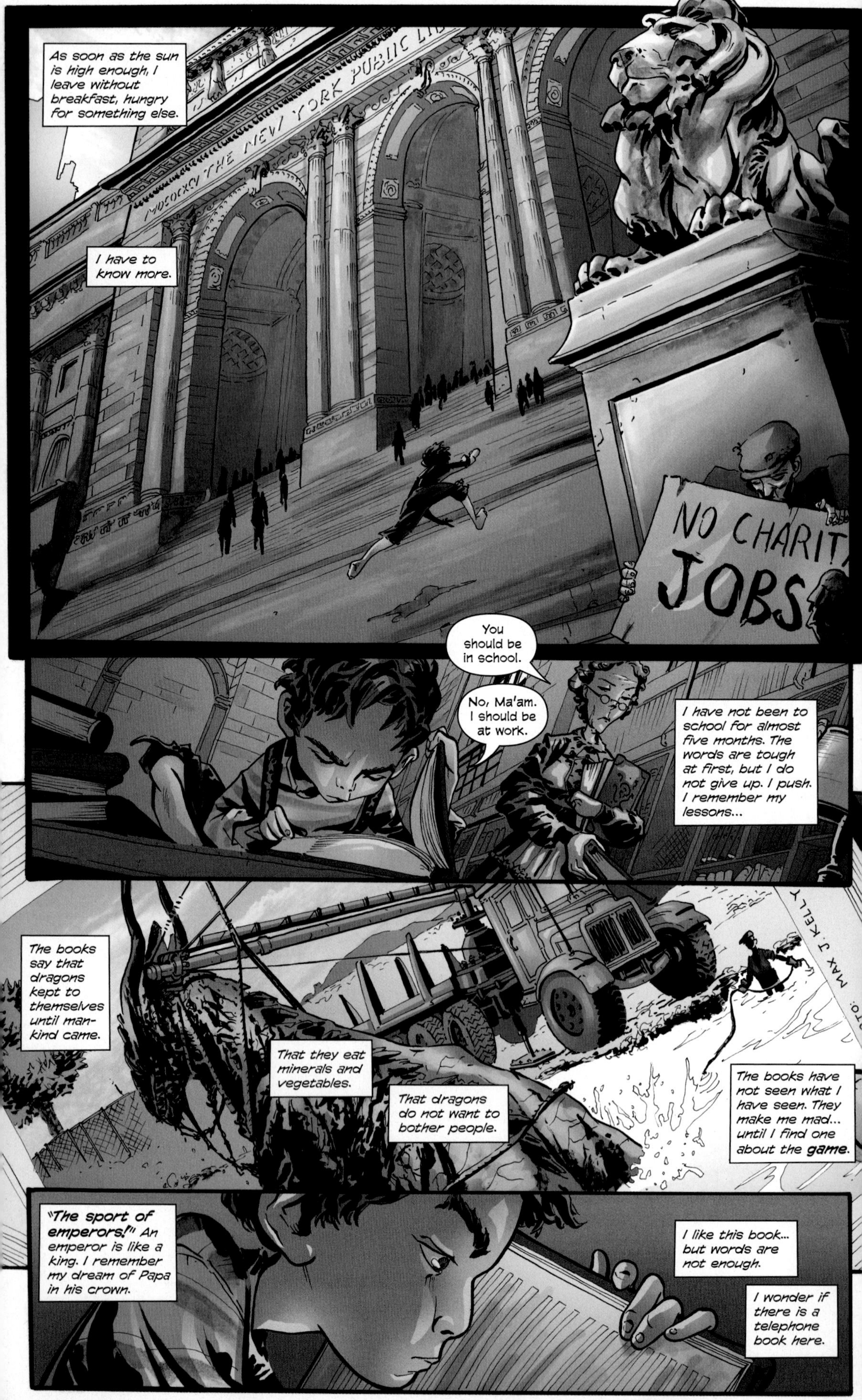
THE NEW YORK PUBLIC LIB
MDCCCCXI
As soon as the sun is high enough, I leave without breakfast, hungry for something else.
I have to know more.
NO CHARIT
JOBS
You should be in school.
No, Ma'am. I should be at work.
I have not been to school for almost five months. The words are tough at first, but I do not give up. I push. I remember my lessons...
The books say that dragons kept to themselves until man-kind came.
That they eat minerals and vegetables.
That dragons do not want to bother people.
MAX J. KELLY
The books have not seen what I have seen. They make me mad... until I find one about the **game**.
"**The sport of emperors!**" An emperor is like a king. I remember my dream of Papa in his crown.
I like this book... but words are not enough.
I wonder if there is a telephone book here.

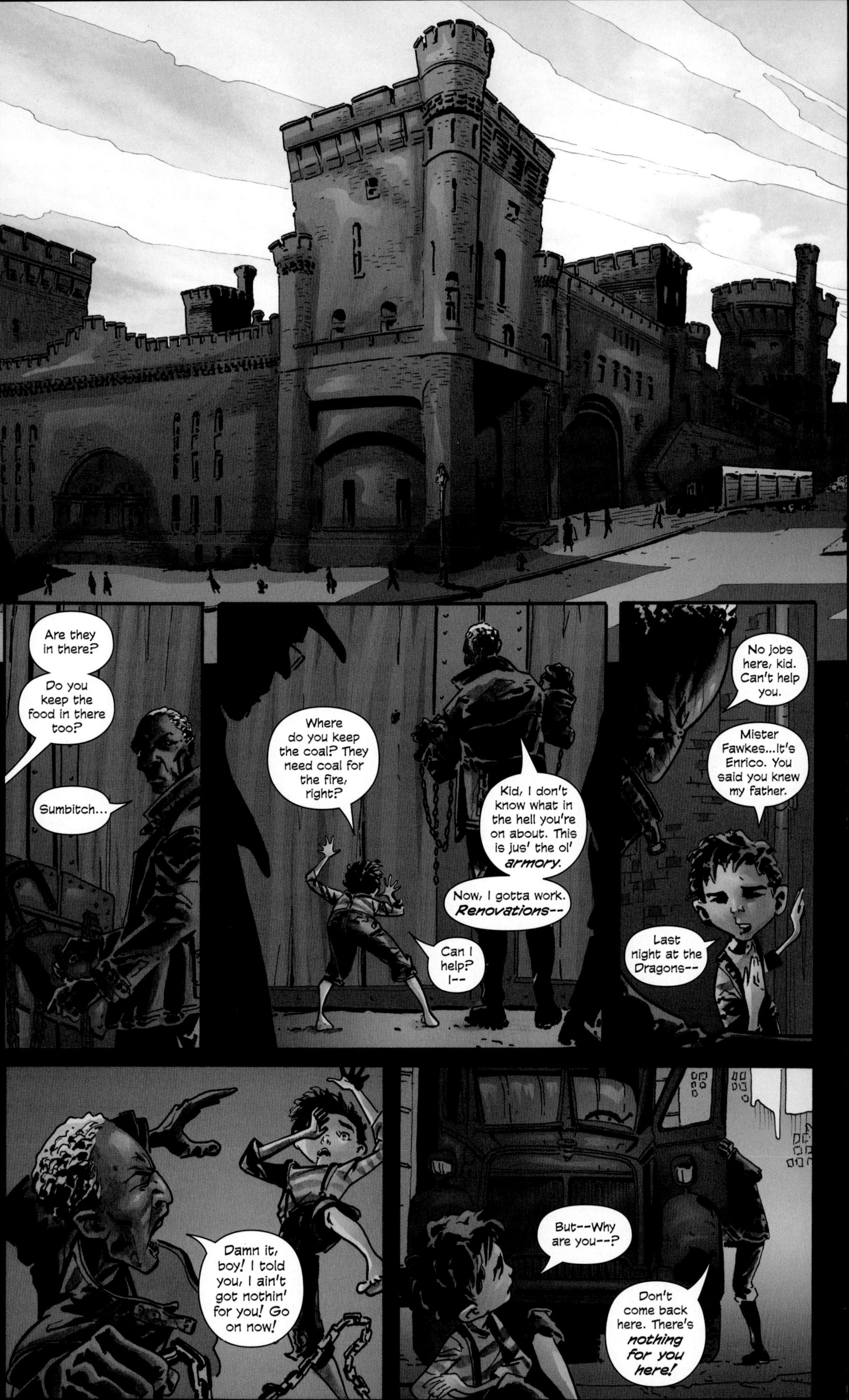
Are they in there?
Do you keep the food in there too?
Sumbitch...
Where do you keep the coal? They need coal for the fire, right?
Kid, I don't know what in the hell you're on about. This is jus' the ol' *armory*.
Now, I gotta work. *Renovations--*
Can I help? I--
No jobs here, kid. Can't help you.
Mister Fawkes...It's Enrico. You said you knew my father.
Last night at the Dragons--
Damn it, boy! I told you, I ain't got nothin' for you! Go on now!
But--Why are you--?
Don't come back here. There's ***nothing for you here!***

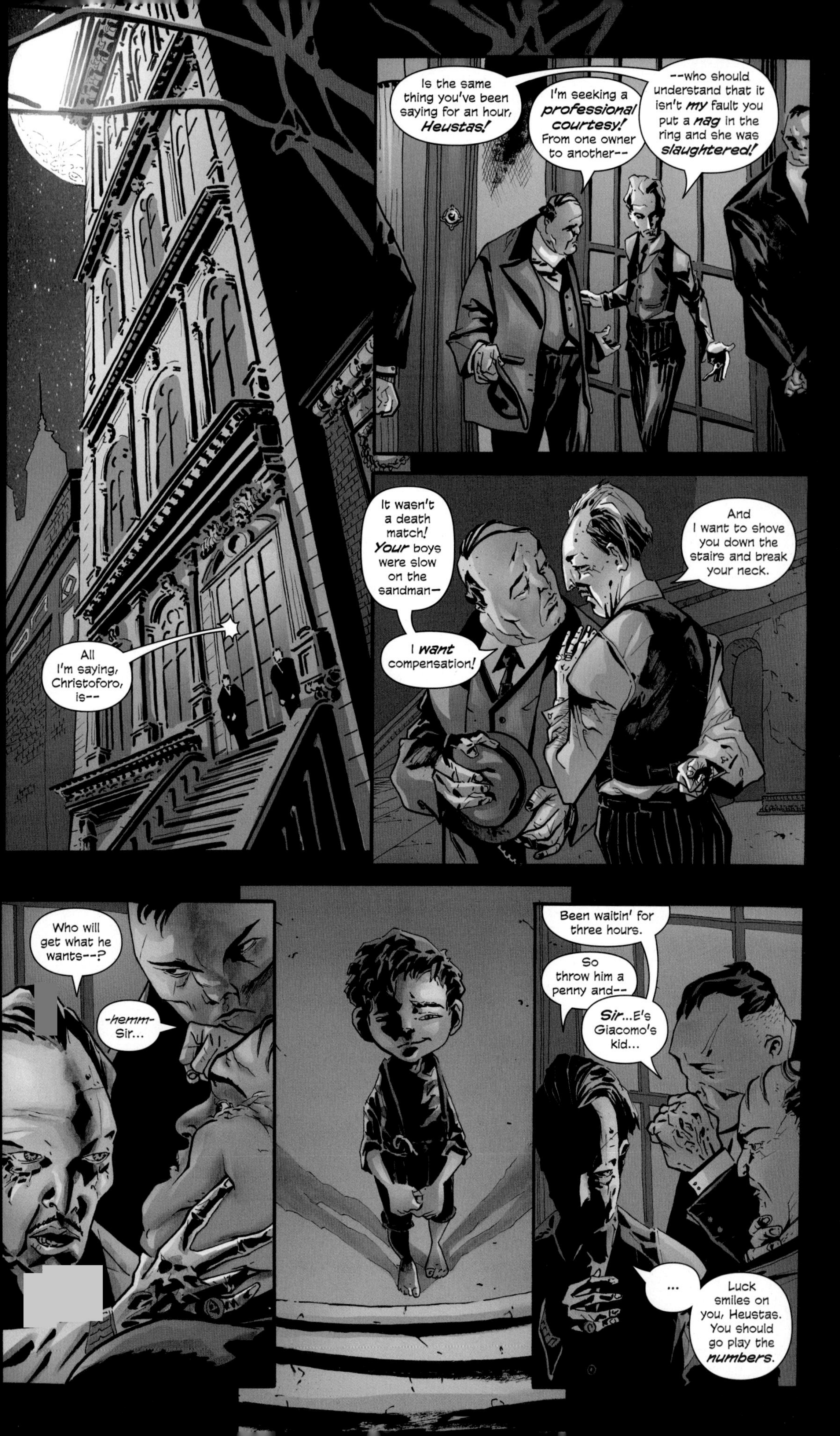

All
I'm saying,
Christoforo,
is--
Is the same
thing you've been
saying for an hour,
Heustas!
I'm seeking a
professional
courtesy!
From one owner
to another--
--who should
understand that it
isn't *my* fault you
put a *nag* in the
ring and she was
slaughtered!
It wasn't
a death
match!
Your boys
were slow
on the
sandman—
I *want*
compensation!
And
I want to shove
you down the
stairs and break
your neck.
Who will
get what he
wants--?
-hemm-
Sir...
Been waitin' for
three hours.
So
throw him a
penny and--
Sir...E's
Giacomo's
kid...
...
Luck
smiles on
you, Heustas.
You should
go play the
numbers.

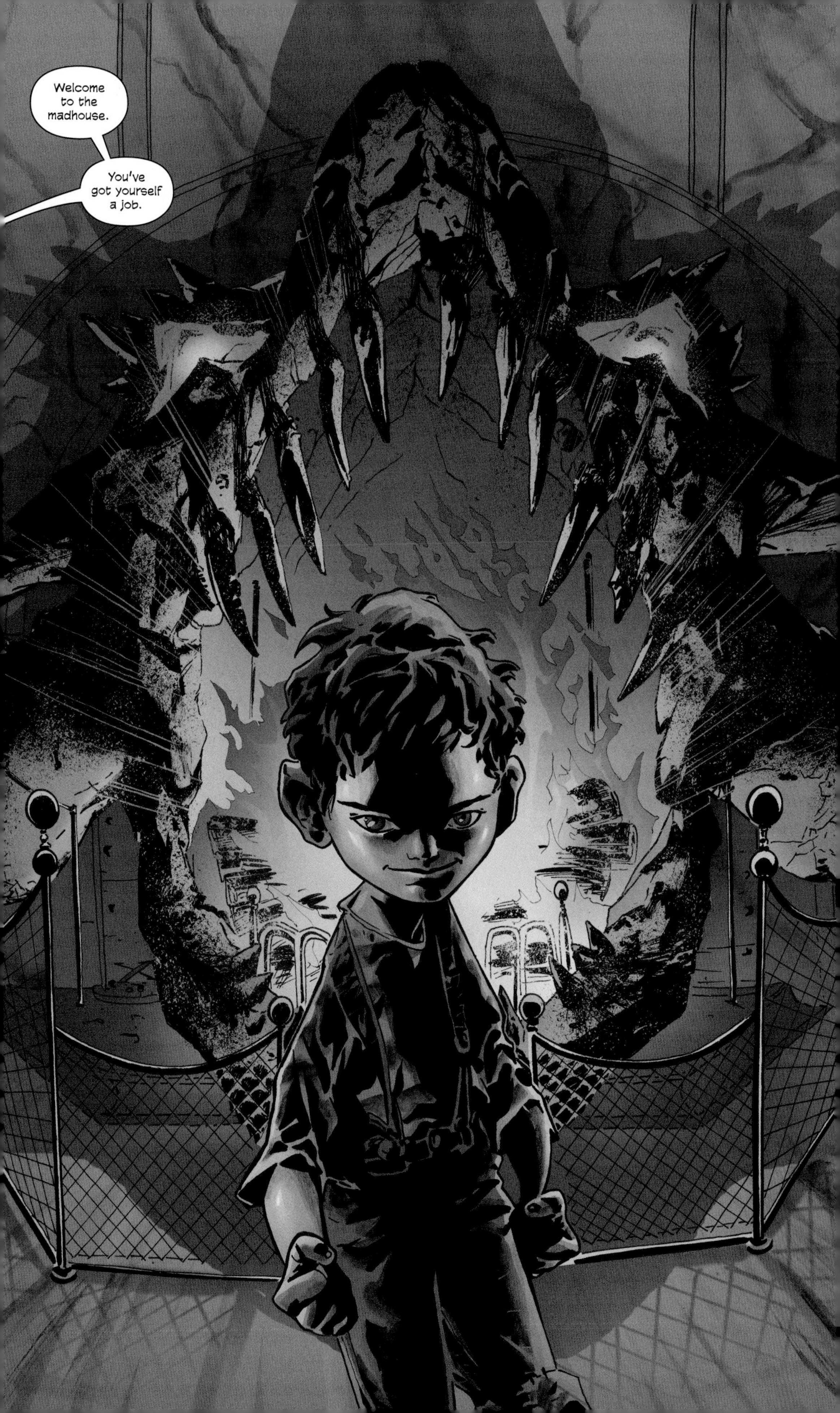
Welcome to the madhouse.
You've got yourself a job.

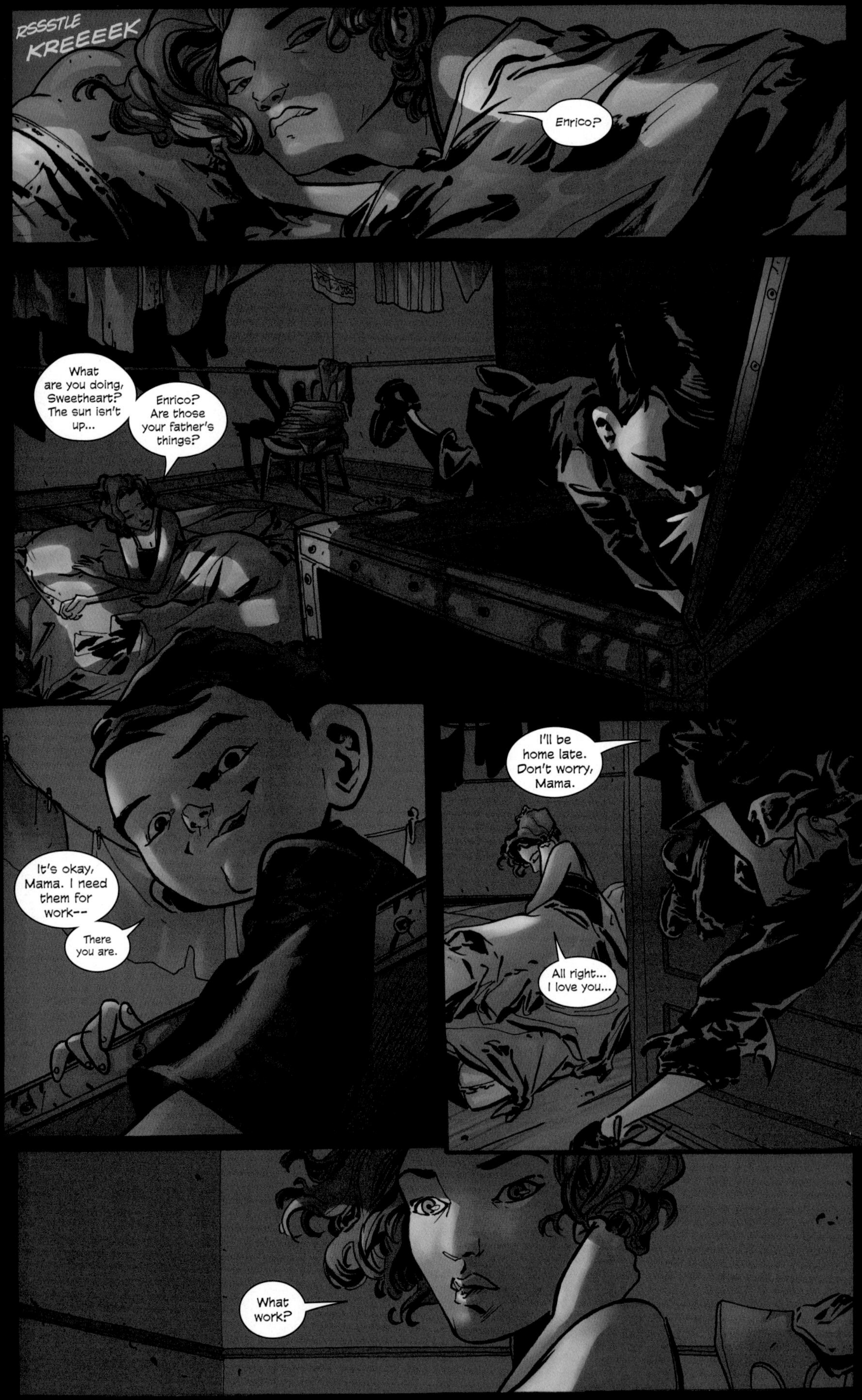
RSSSTLE
KREEEEK
Enrico?
What are you doing, Sweetheart? The sun isn't up...
Enrico? Are those your father's things?
It's okay, Mama. I need them for work--
There you are.
I'll be home late. Don't worry, Mama.
All right... I love you...
What work?

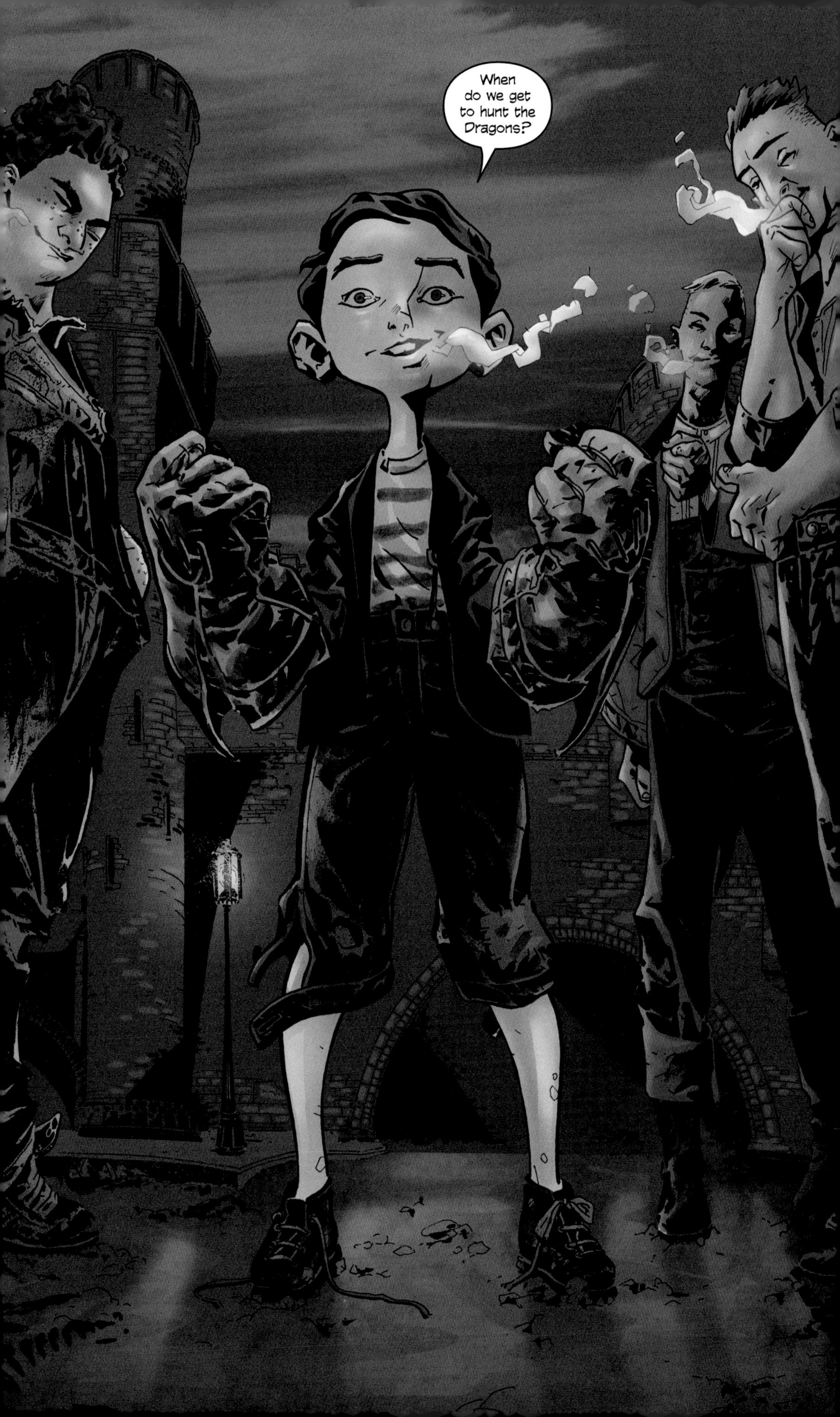
When do we get to hunt the Dragons?

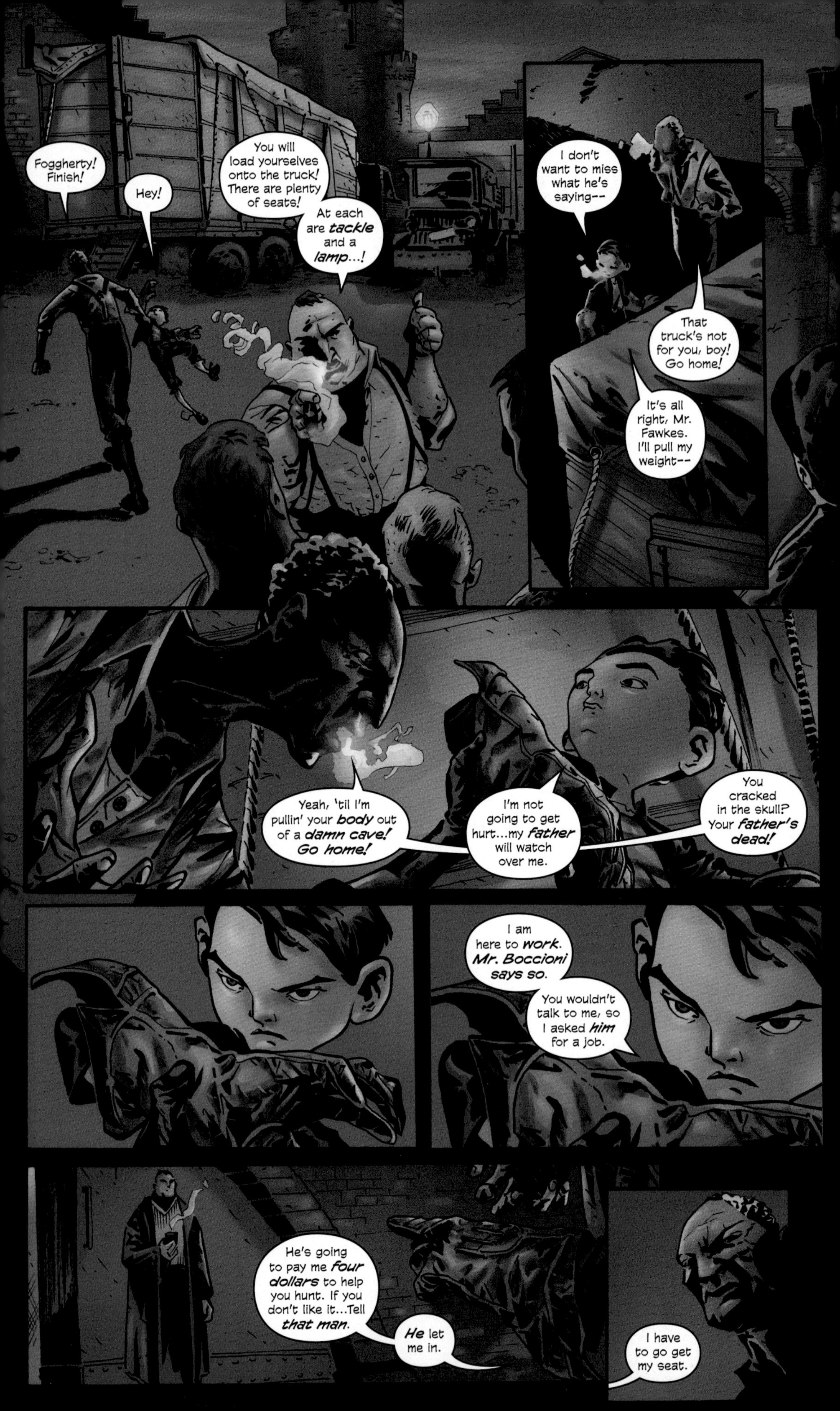

Foggherty! Finish!
Hey!
You will load yourselves onto the truck! There are plenty of seats!
At each are *tackle* and a *lamp*...!
I don't want to miss what he's saying--
That truck's not for you, boy! Go home!
It's all right, Mr. Fawkes. I'll pull my weight--
Yeah, 'til I'm pullin' your *body* out of a *damn cave! Go home!*
I'm not going to get hurt...my *father* will watch over me.
You cracked in the skull? Your *father's dead!*
I am here to *work*. *Mr. Boccioni says so*.
You wouldn't talk to me, so I asked *him* for a job.
He's going to pay me *four dollars* to help you hunt. If you don't like it...Tell *that man*.
He let me in.
I have to go get my seat.

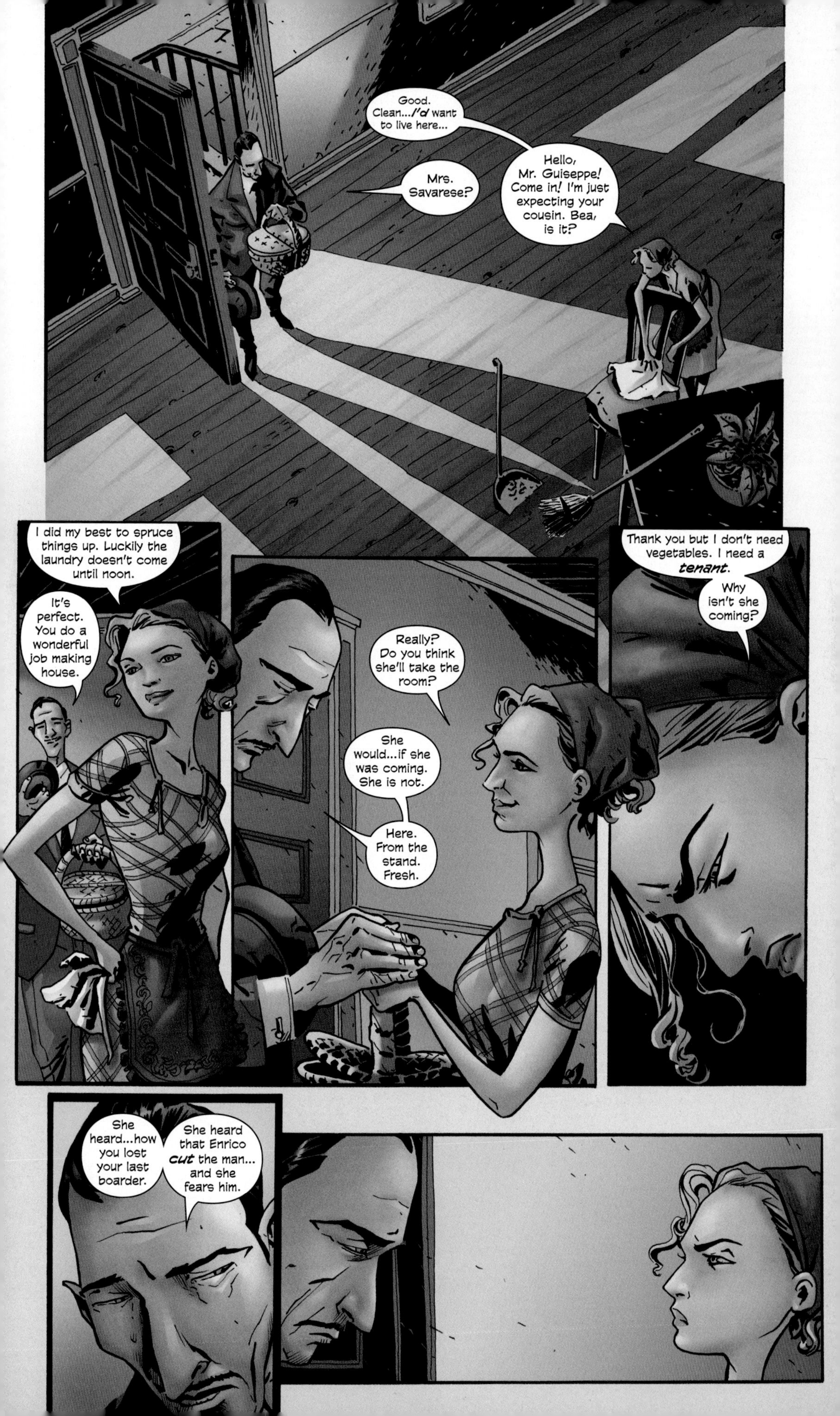
Good. Clean...I'd want to live here...
Mrs. Savarese?
Hello, Mr. Guiseppe! Come in! I'm just expecting your cousin. Bea, is it?
I did my best to spruce things up. Luckily the laundry doesn't come until noon.
It's perfect. You do a wonderful job making house.
Really? Do you think she'll take the room?
She would...if she was coming. She is not.
Here. From the stand. Fresh.
Thank you but I don't need vegetables. I need a *tenant*.
Why isn't she coming?
She heard...how you lost your last boarder.
She heard that Enrico *cut* the man... and she fears him.

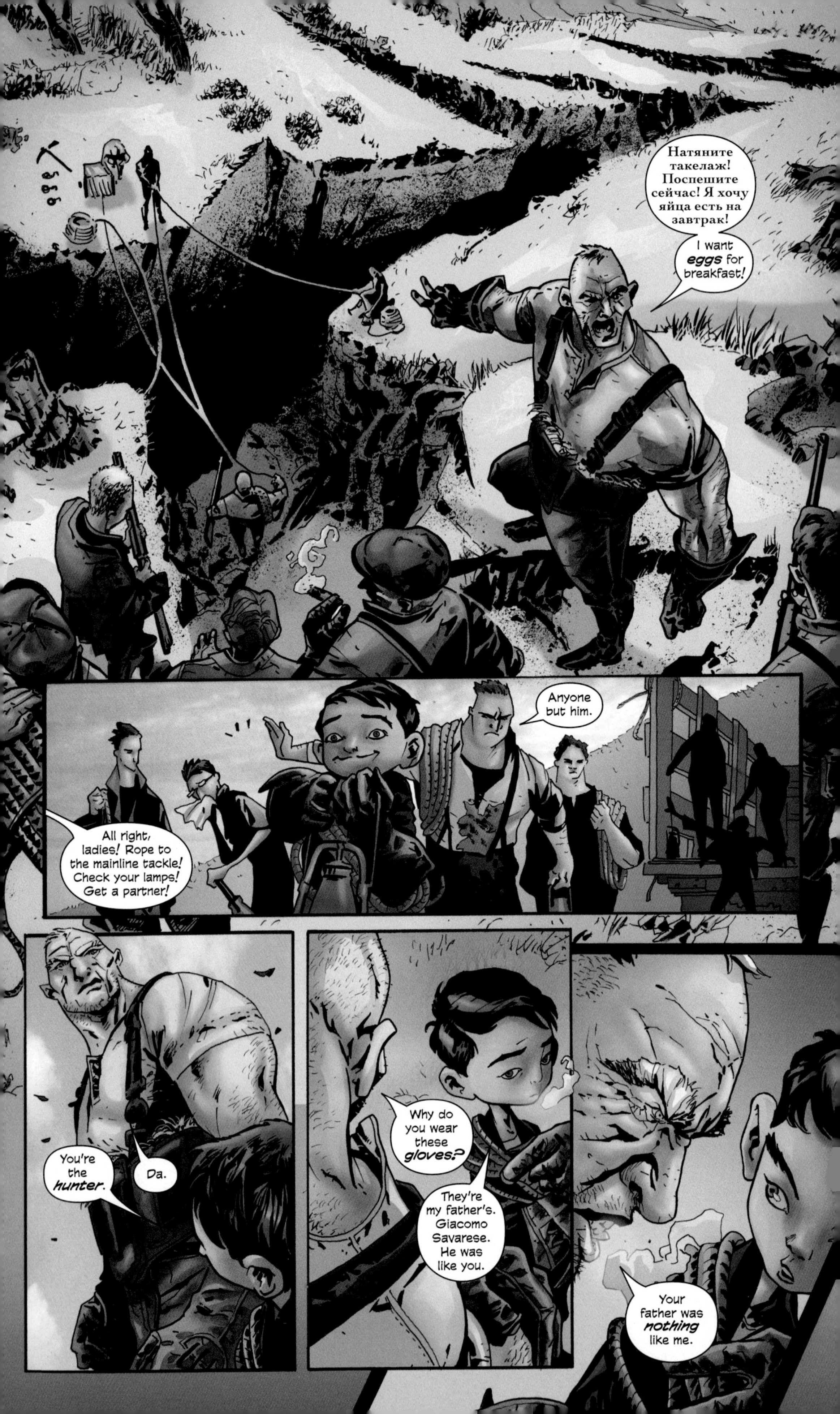

Натяните такелаж! Поспешите сейчас! Я хочу яйца есть на завтрак!
I want eggs for breakfast!
All right, ladies! Rope to the mainline tackle! Check your lamps! Get a partner!
Anyone but him.
You're the hunter.
Da.
Why do you wear these gloves?
They're my father's. Giacomo Savarese. He was like you.
Your father was nothing like me.

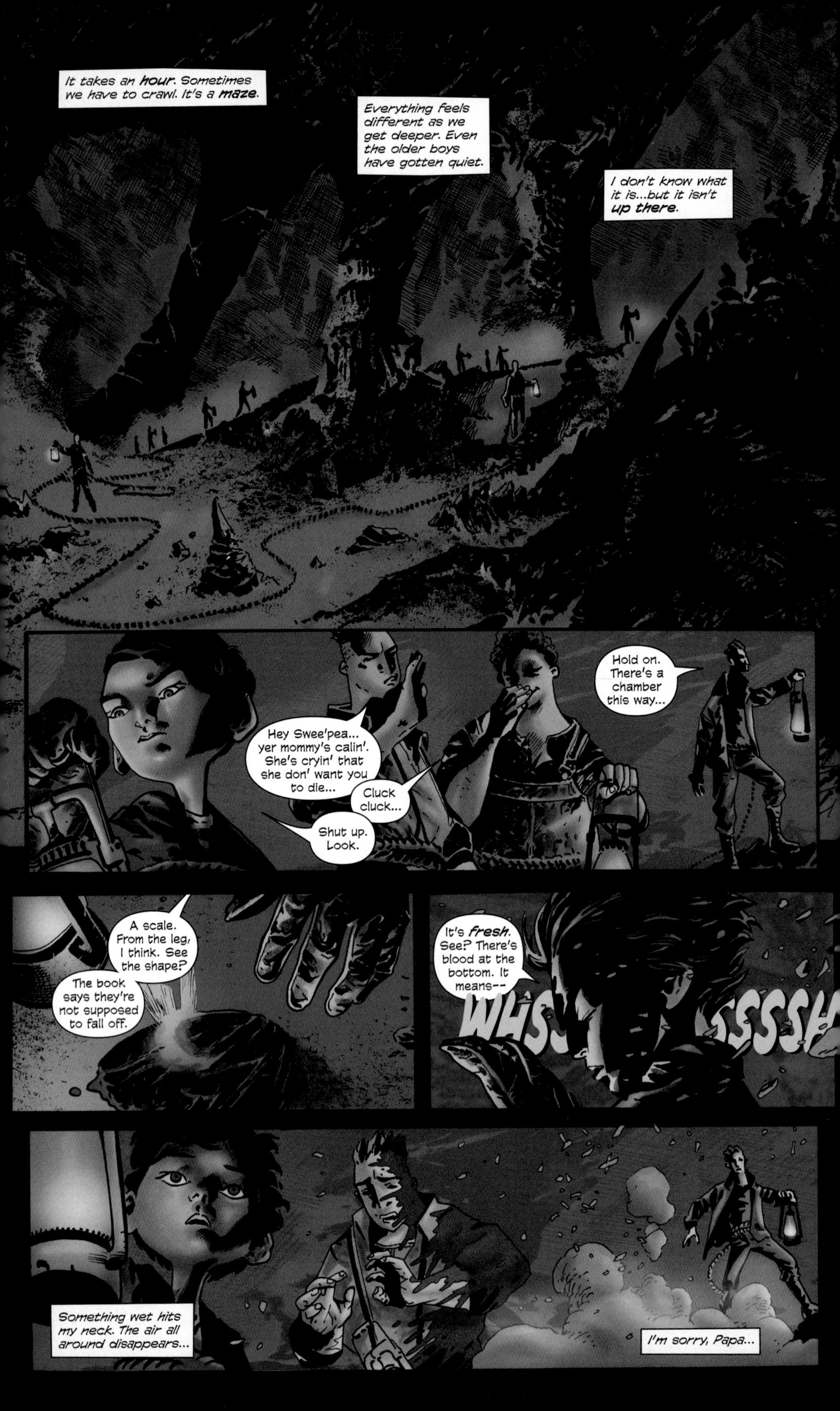
It takes an **hour**. Sometimes we have to crawl. It's a **maze**.
Everything feels different as we get deeper. Even the older boys have gotten quiet.
I don't know what it is...but it isn't **up there**.
Hold on. There's a chamber this way...
Hey Swee'pea... yer mommy's calin'. She's cryin' that she don' want you to die...
Cluck cluck...
Shut up. Look.
A scale. From the leg, I think. See the shape?
The book says they're not supposed to fall off.
It's *fresh*. See? There's blood at the bottom. It means--
WHSSSSSH
Something wet hits my neck. The air all around disappears...
I'm sorry, Papa...

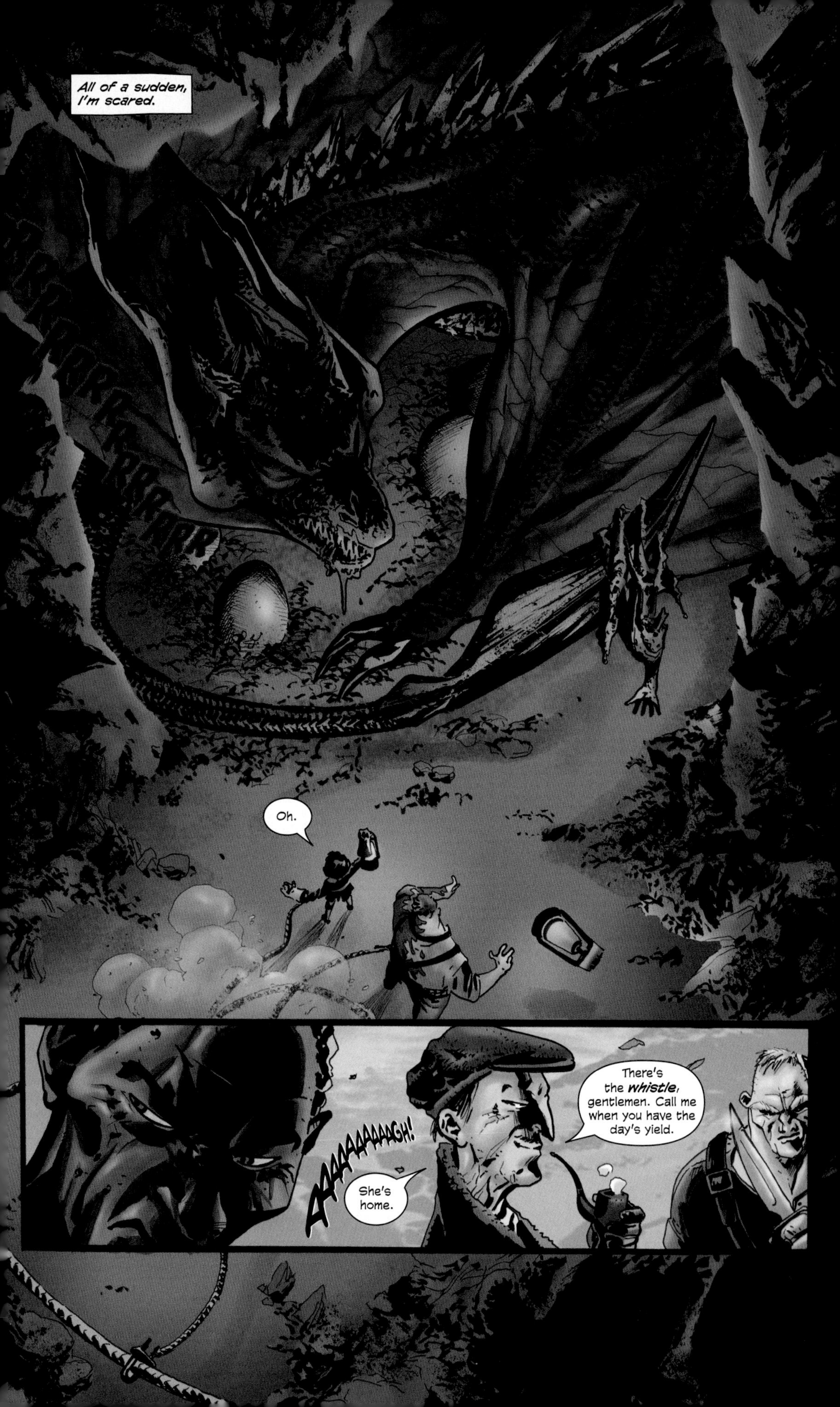
All of a sudden, I'm scared.
Oh.
AAAAAAAAAAGH!
She's home.
There's the *whistle*, gentlemen. Call me when you have the day's yield.

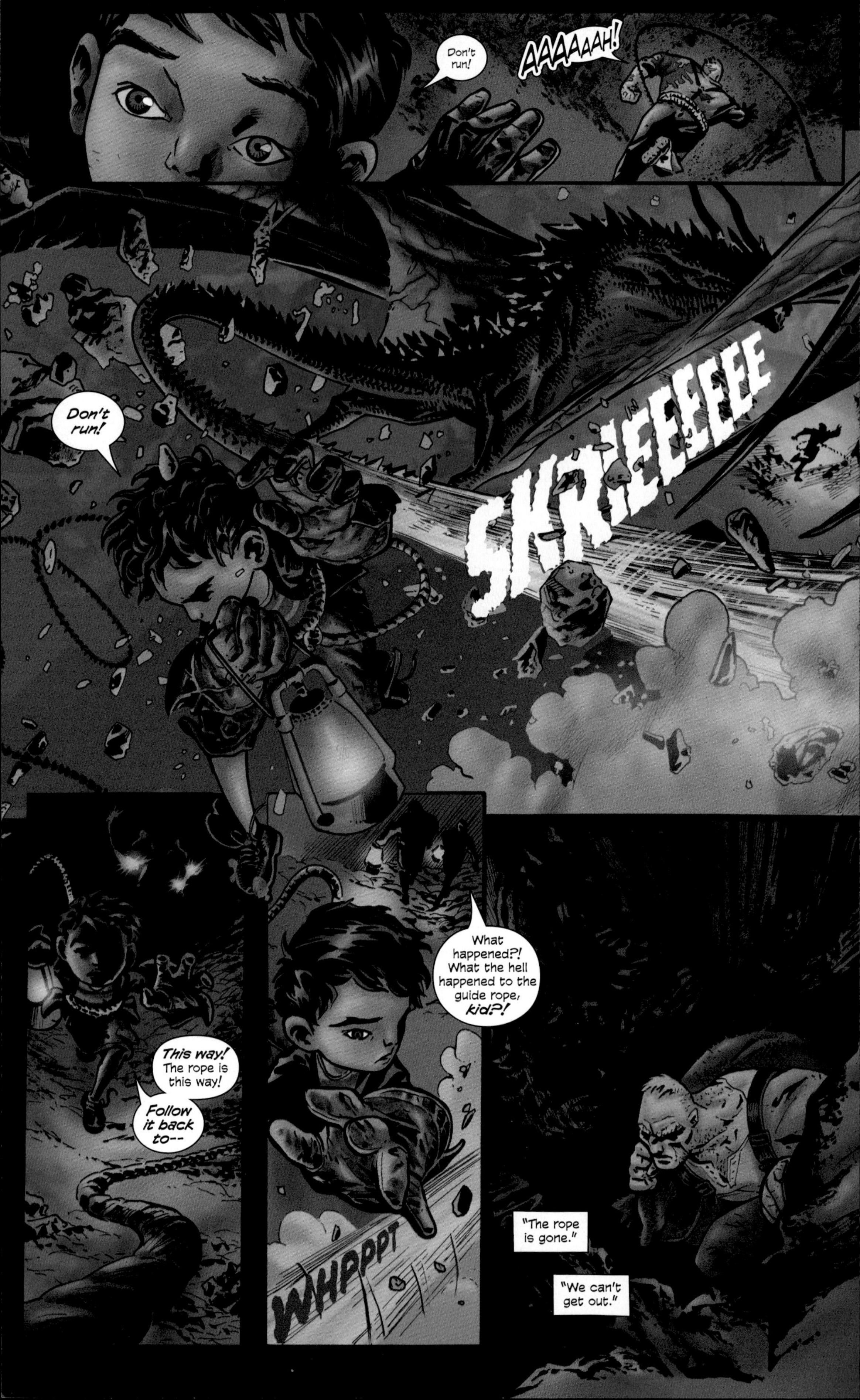

Don't run!
AAAAAAH!
Don't run!
SKREEEEEEE
This way! The rope is this way!
Follow it back to--
What happened?! What the hell happened to the guide rope, kid?!
WHPPPT
"The rope is gone."
"We can't get out."

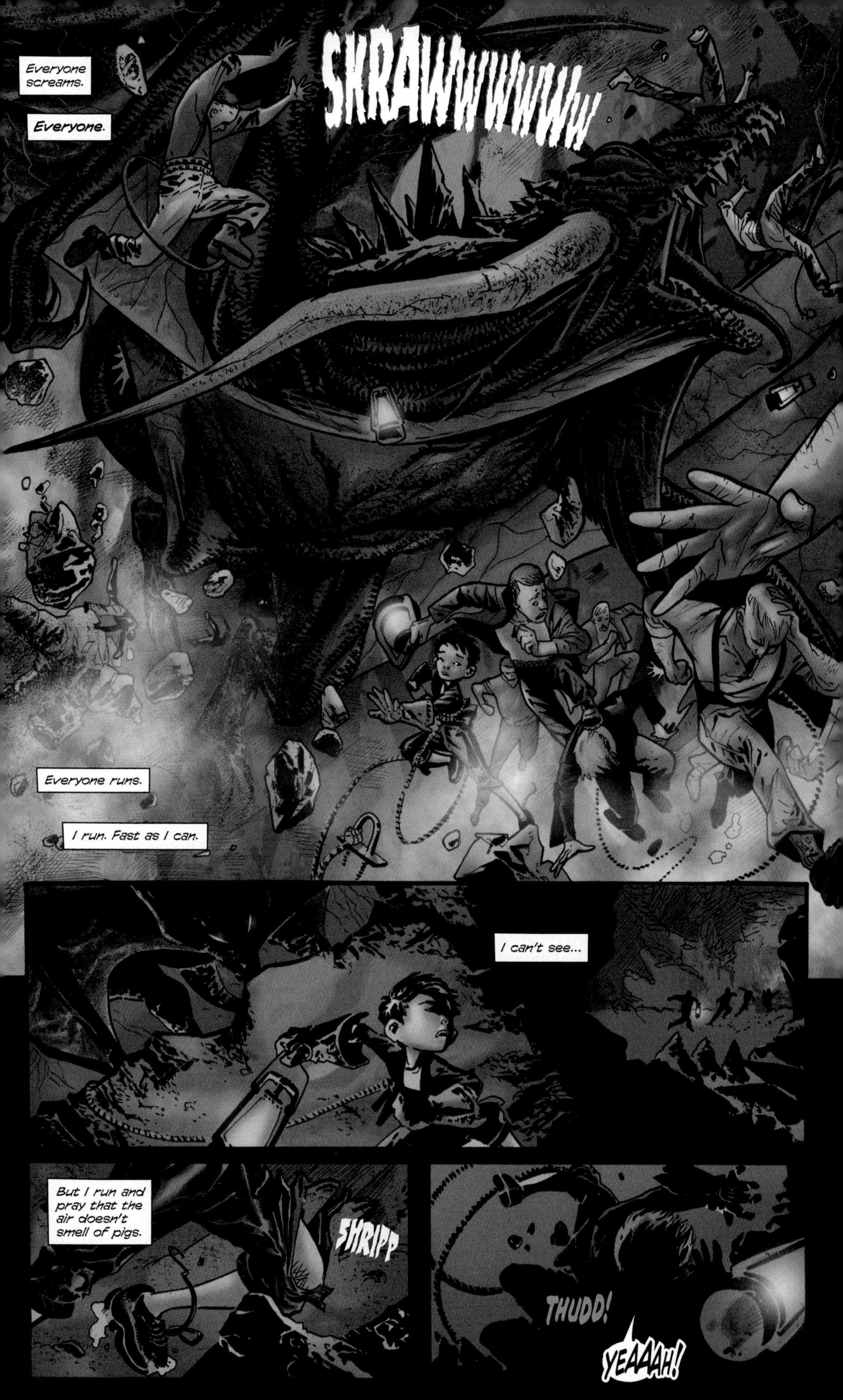
Everyone screams.
Everyone.
SKRAWWWWWW
Everyone runs.
I run. Fast as I can.
I can't see...
But I run and pray that the air doesn't smell of pigs.
SHRIPP
THUDD!
YEAAAH!

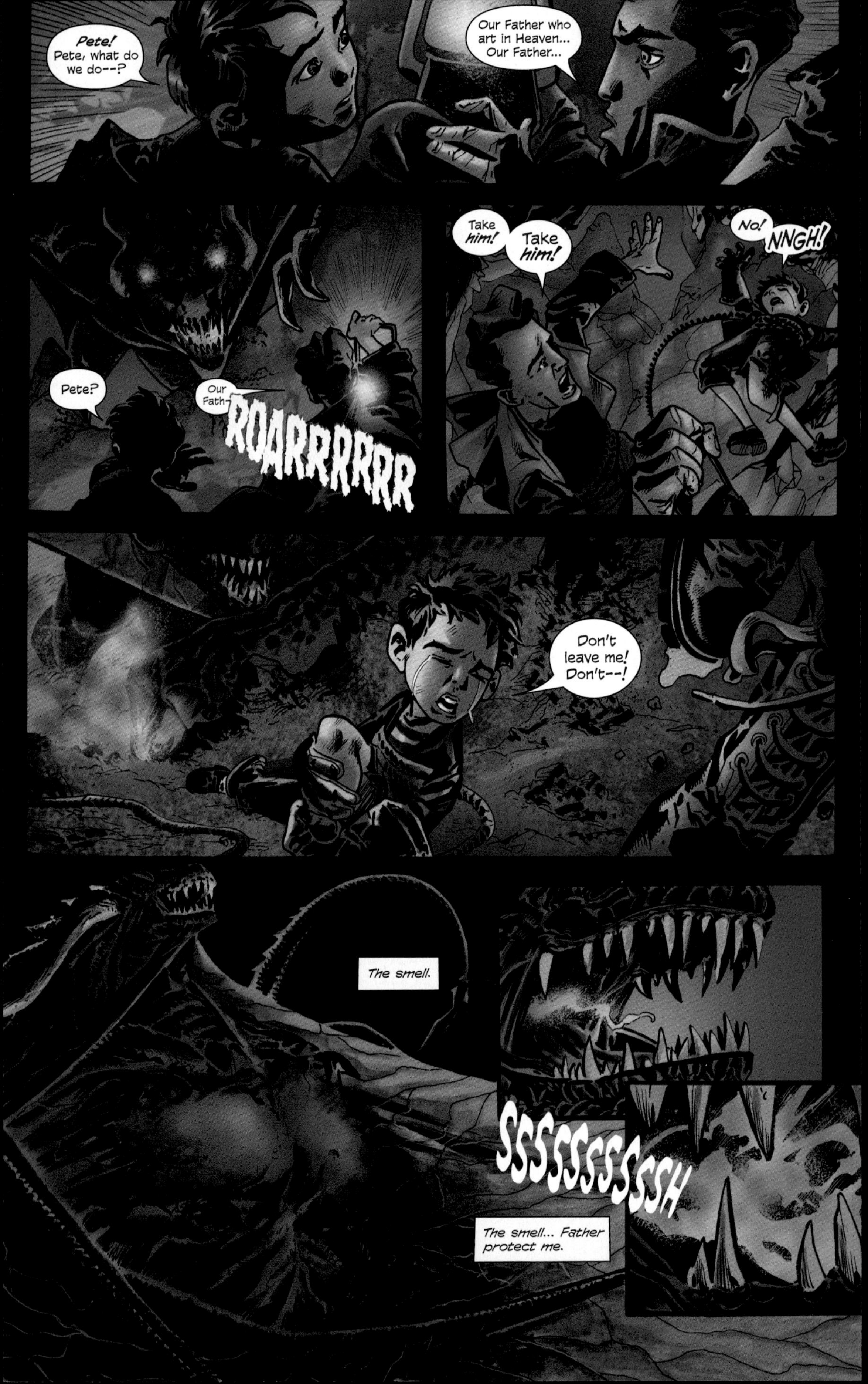

Pete! Pete, what do we do--?
Our Father who art in Heaven... Our Father...
Pete?
Our Fath--
ROARRRRRR
Take him!
Take him!
No!
NNGH!
Don't leave me! Don't--!
The smell.
SSSSSSSSSH
The smell... Father protect me.

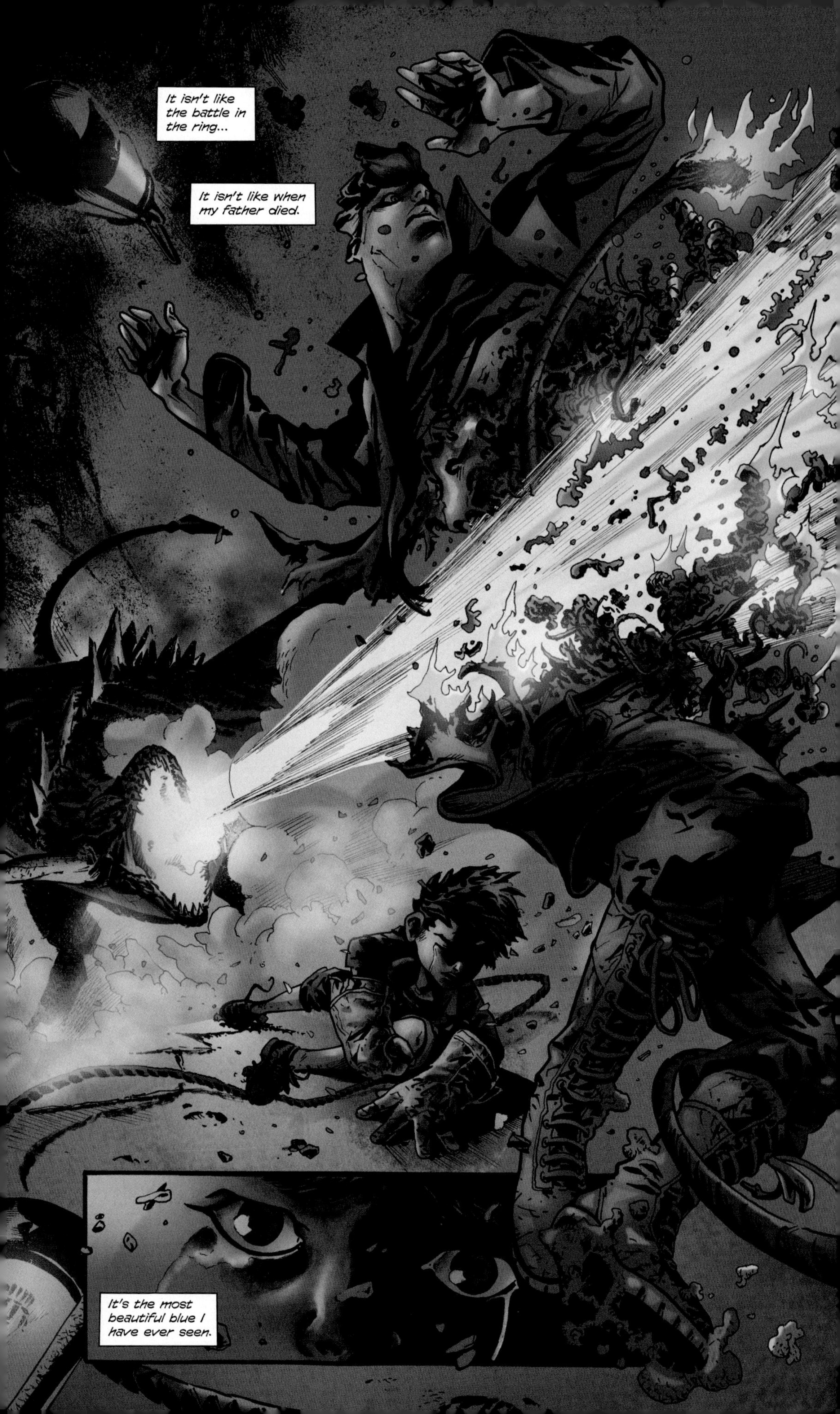
It isn't like the battle in the ring...
It isn't like when my father died.
It's the most beautiful blue I have ever seen.

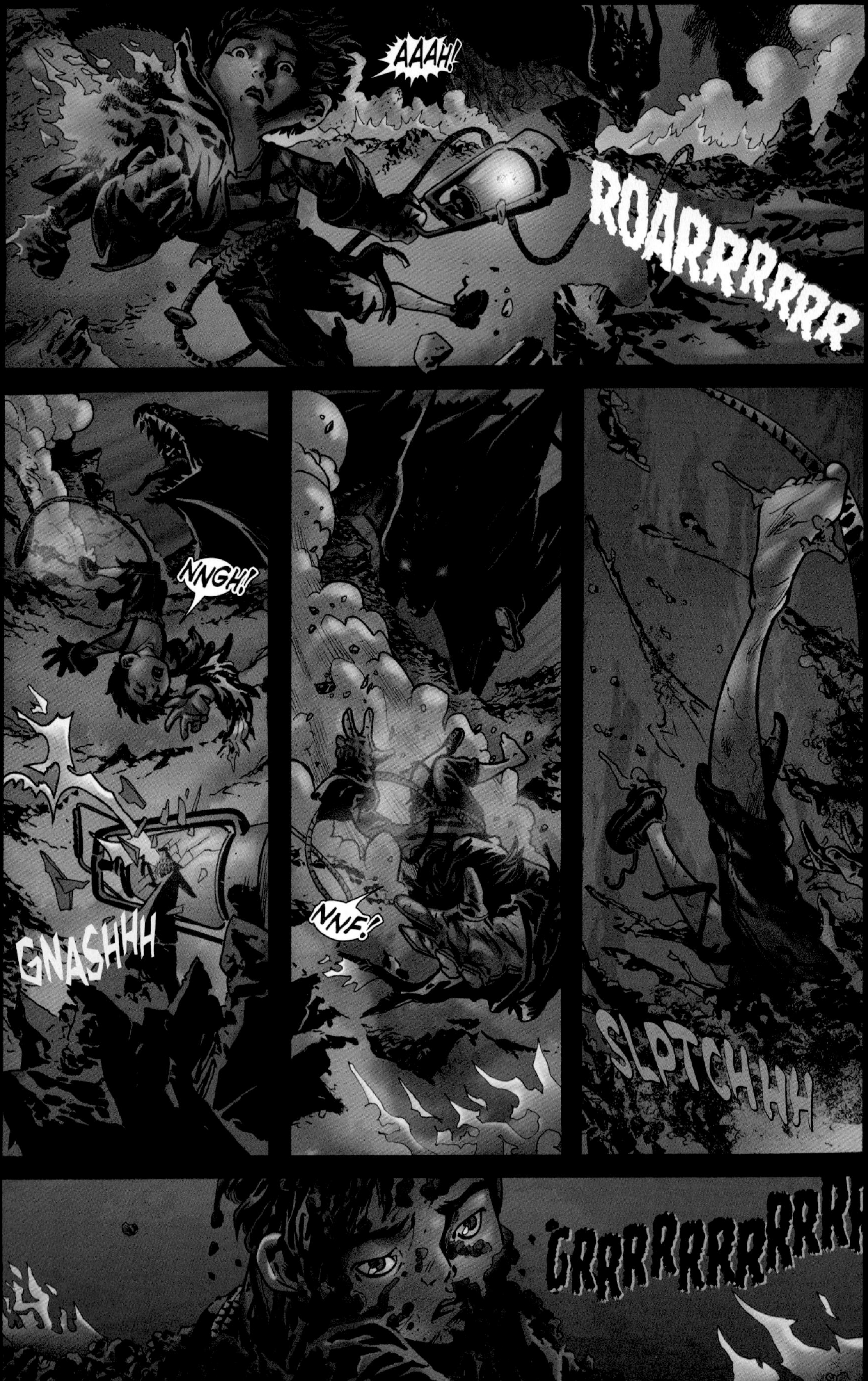
AAAH!
ROARRRRRRR
NNGH!
GNASHHH
NNF!
SLPTCHHH
GRRRRRRRRRRR

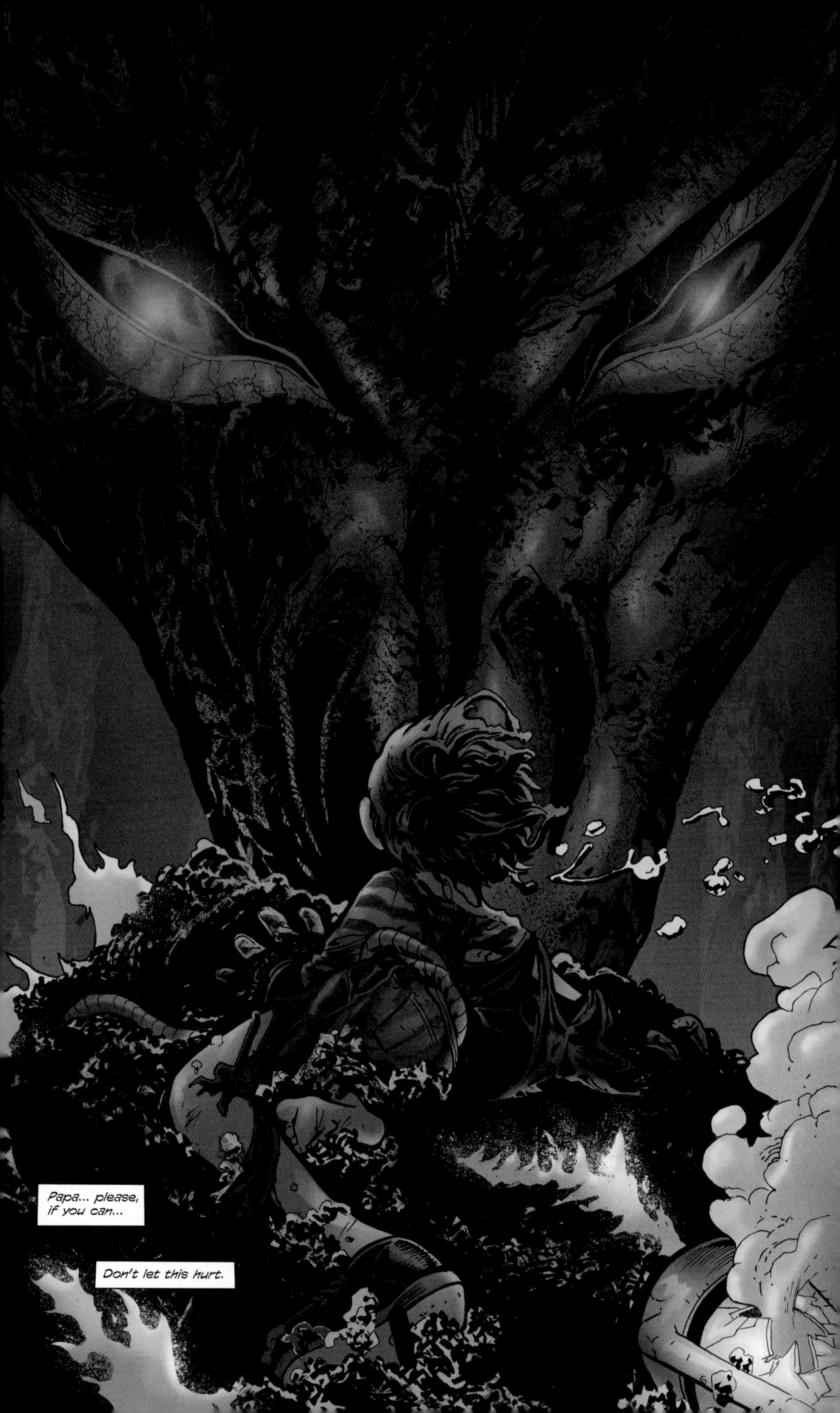
Papa... please, if you can...
Don't let this hurt.

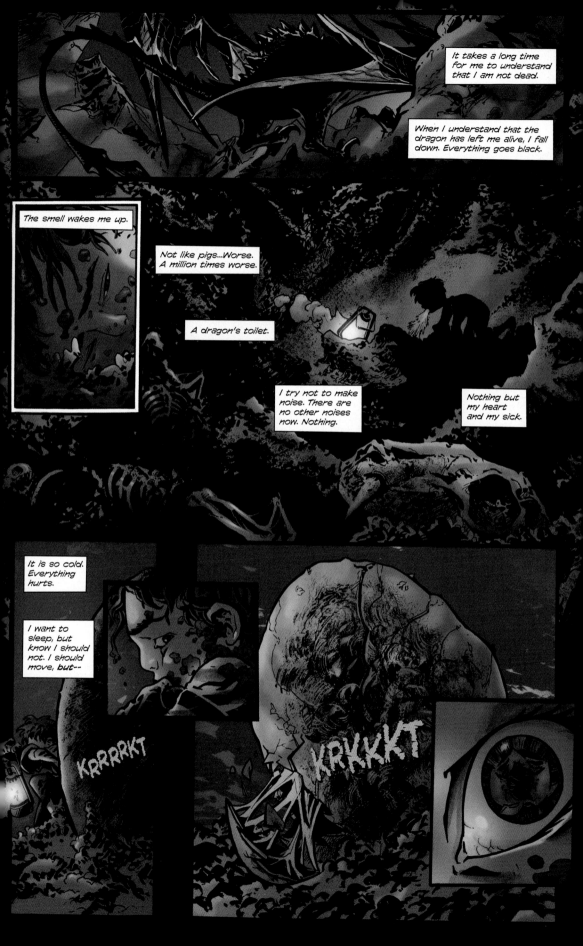

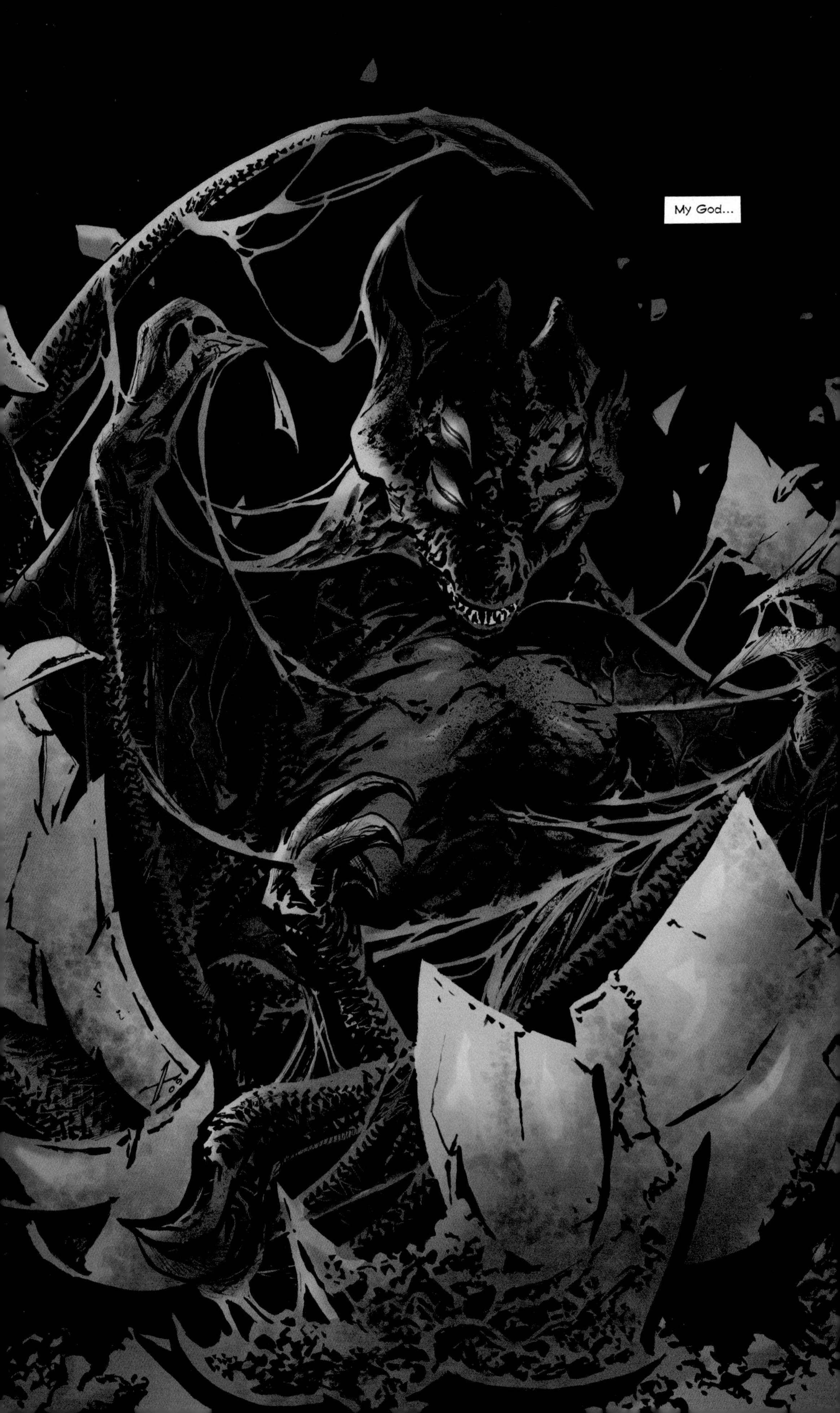
My God...

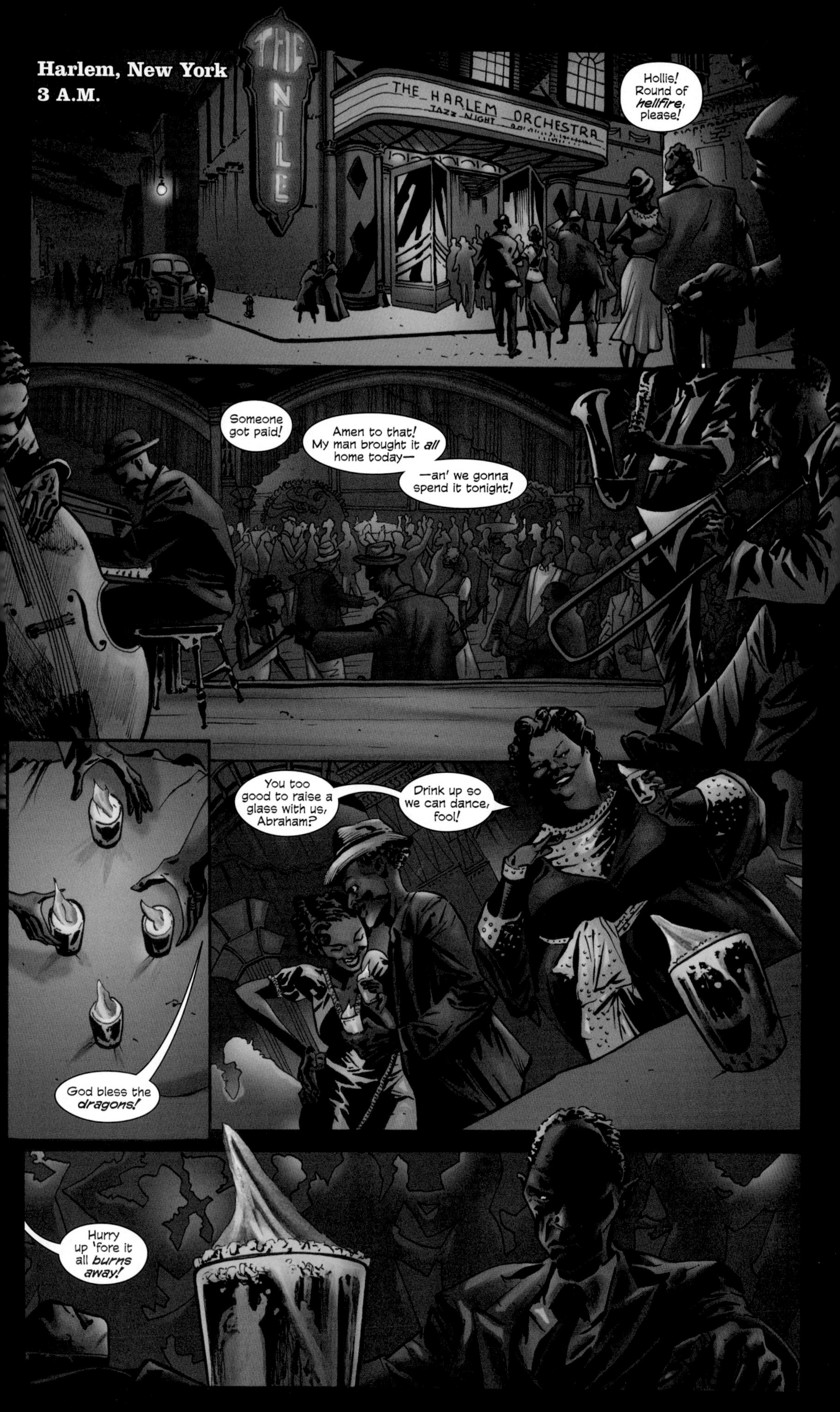
Harlem, New York
3 A.M.
THE NILE
THE HARLEM ORCHESTRA
JAZZ NIGHT
Hollis! Round of *hellfire*, please!
Someone got paid!
Amen to that! My man brought it *all* home today—
—an' we gonna spend it tonight!
You too good to raise a glass with us, Abraham?
Drink up so we can dance, fool!
God bless the *dragons!*
Hurry up 'fore it all *burns away!*

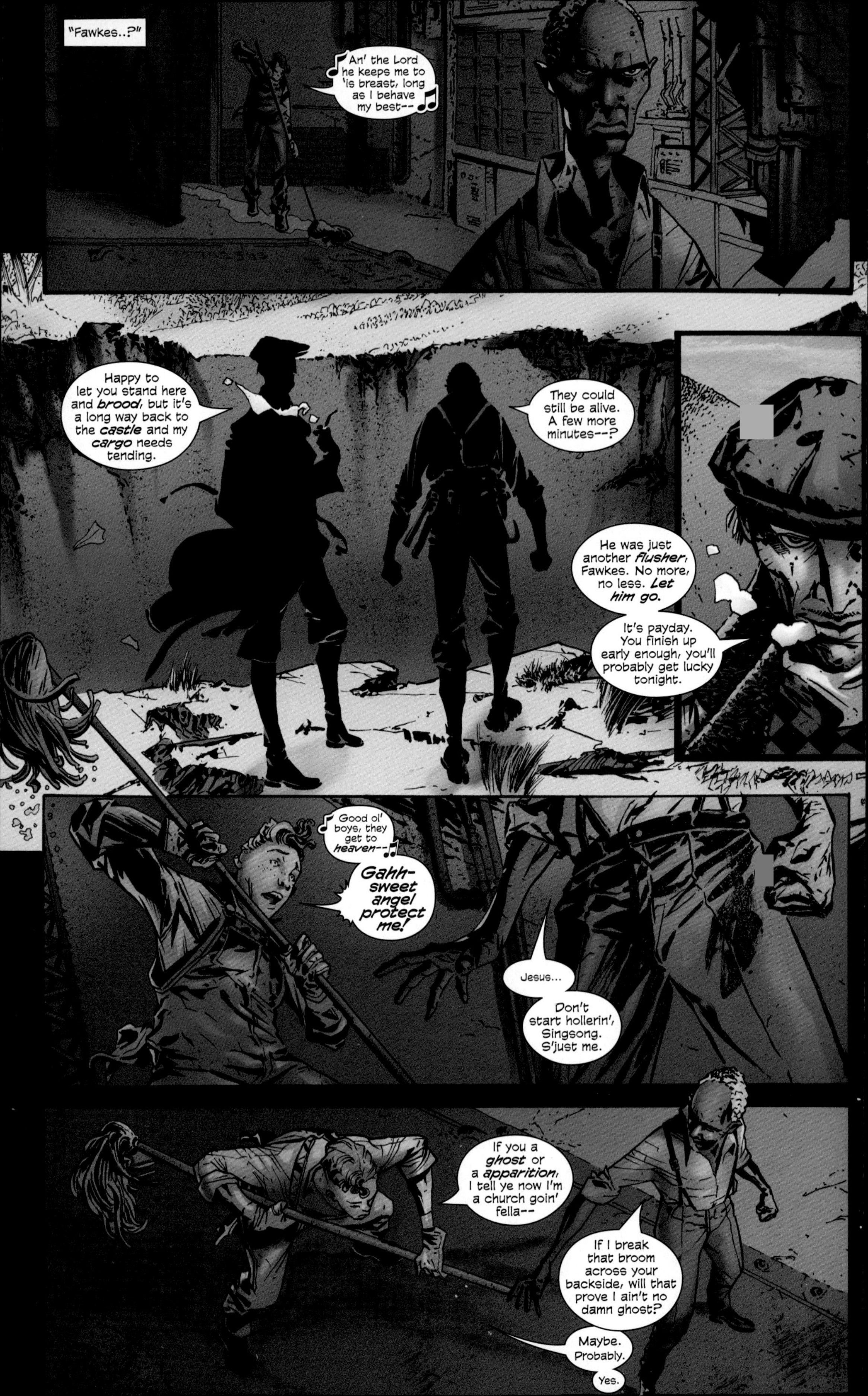
"Fawkes..?"
An' the Lord he keeps me to 'is breast, long as I behave my best--
Happy to let you stand here and *brood*, but it's a long way back to the *castle* and my *cargo* needs tending.
They could still be alive. A few more minutes--?
He was just another *flusher*, Fawkes. No more, no less. *Let him go.*
It's payday. You finish up early enough, you'll probably get lucky tonight.
Good ol' boys, they get to *heaven*--
Gahh- sweet angel protect me!
Jesus...
Don't start hollerin', Singsong. S'just me.
If you a *ghost* or a *apparition*, I tell ye now I'm a church goin' fella--
If I break that broom across your backside, will that prove I ain't no damn ghost?
Maybe. Probably.
Yes.

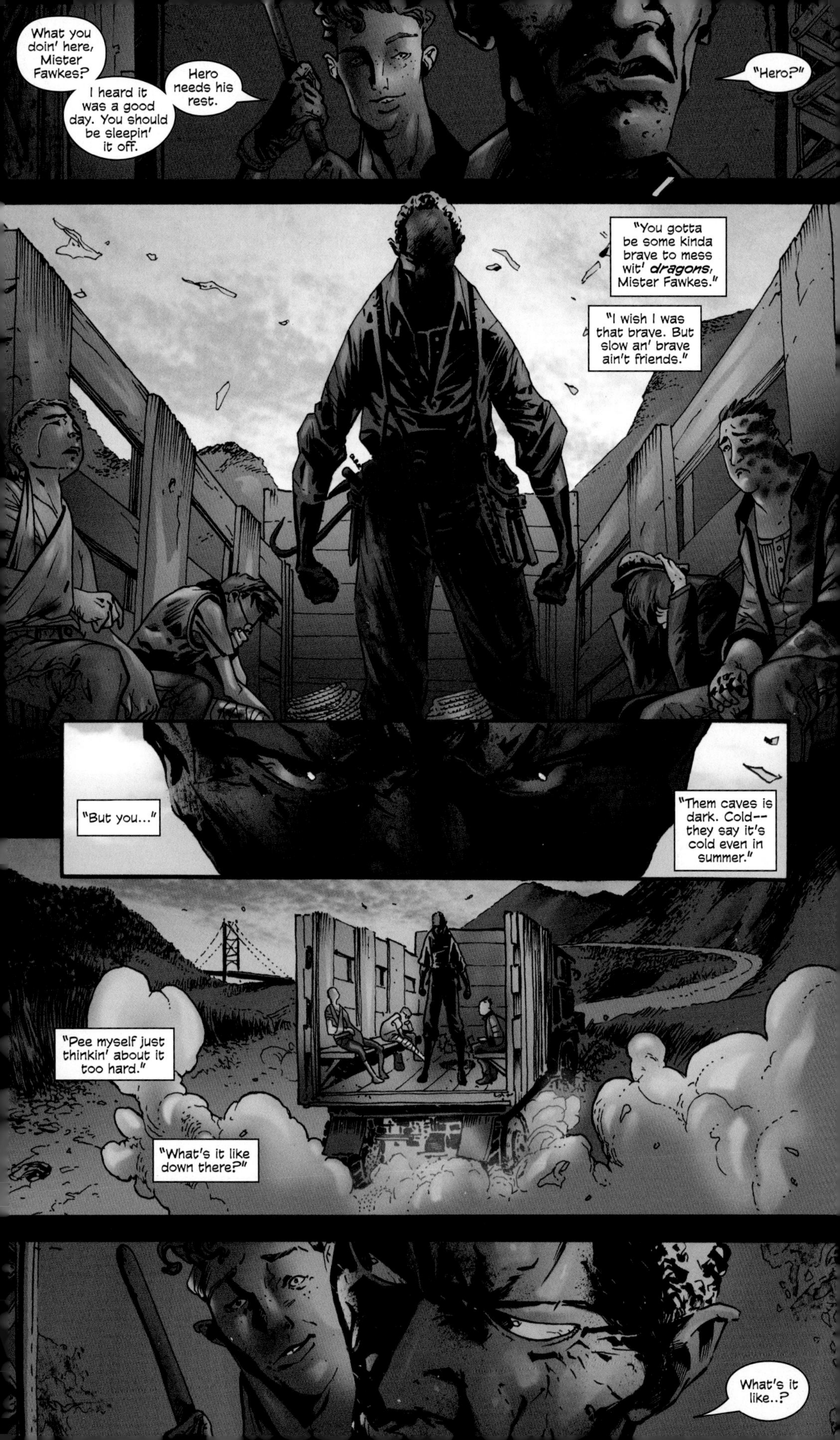
What you doin' here, Mister Fawkes?
I heard it was a good day. You should be sleepin' it off.
Hero needs his rest.
"Hero?"
"You gotta be some kinda brave to mess wit' *dragons*, Mister Fawkes."
"I wish I was that brave. But slow an' brave ain't friends."
"But you..."
"Them caves is dark. Cold-- they say it's cold even in summer."
"Pee myself just thinkin' about it too hard."
"What's it like down there?"
What's it like..?

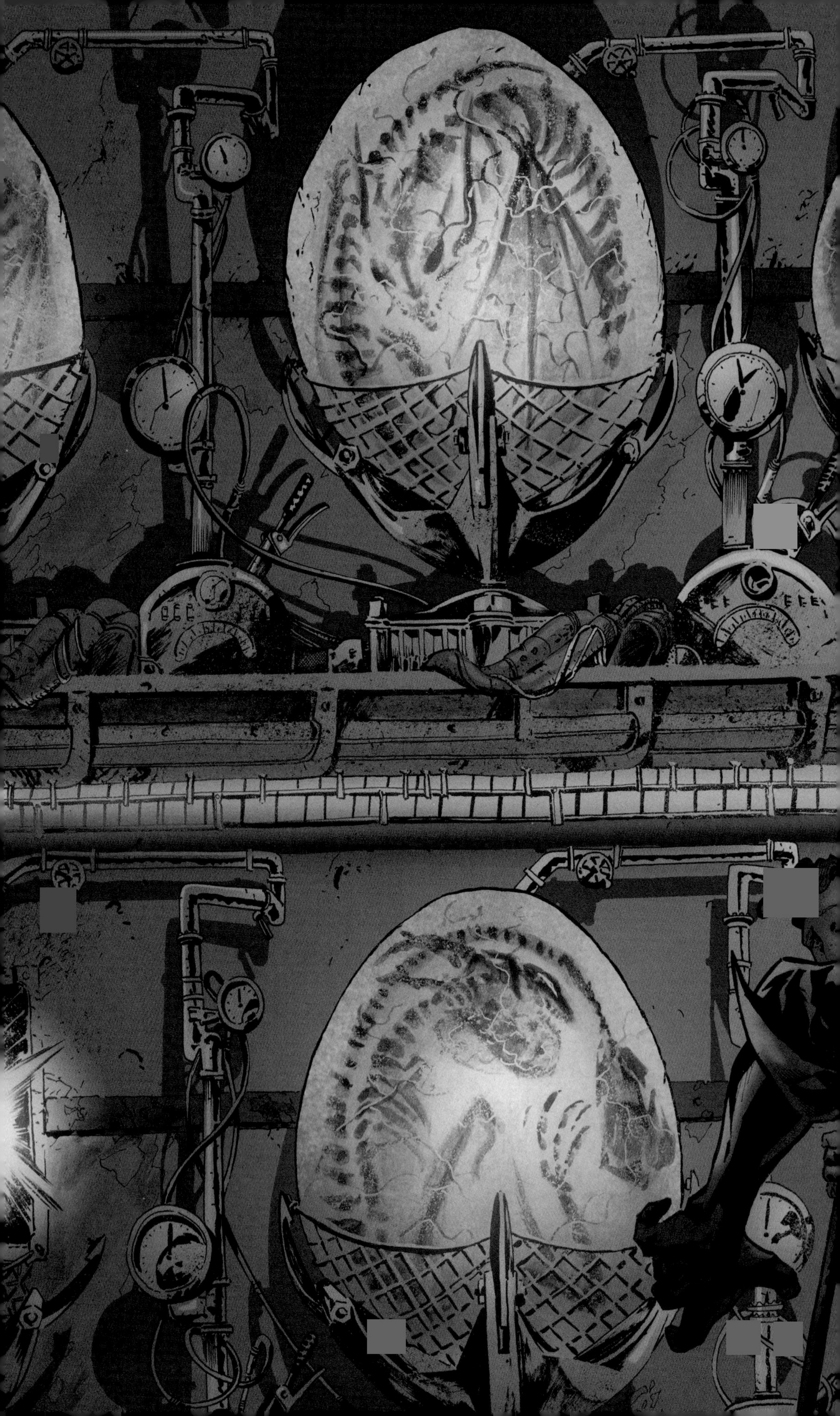

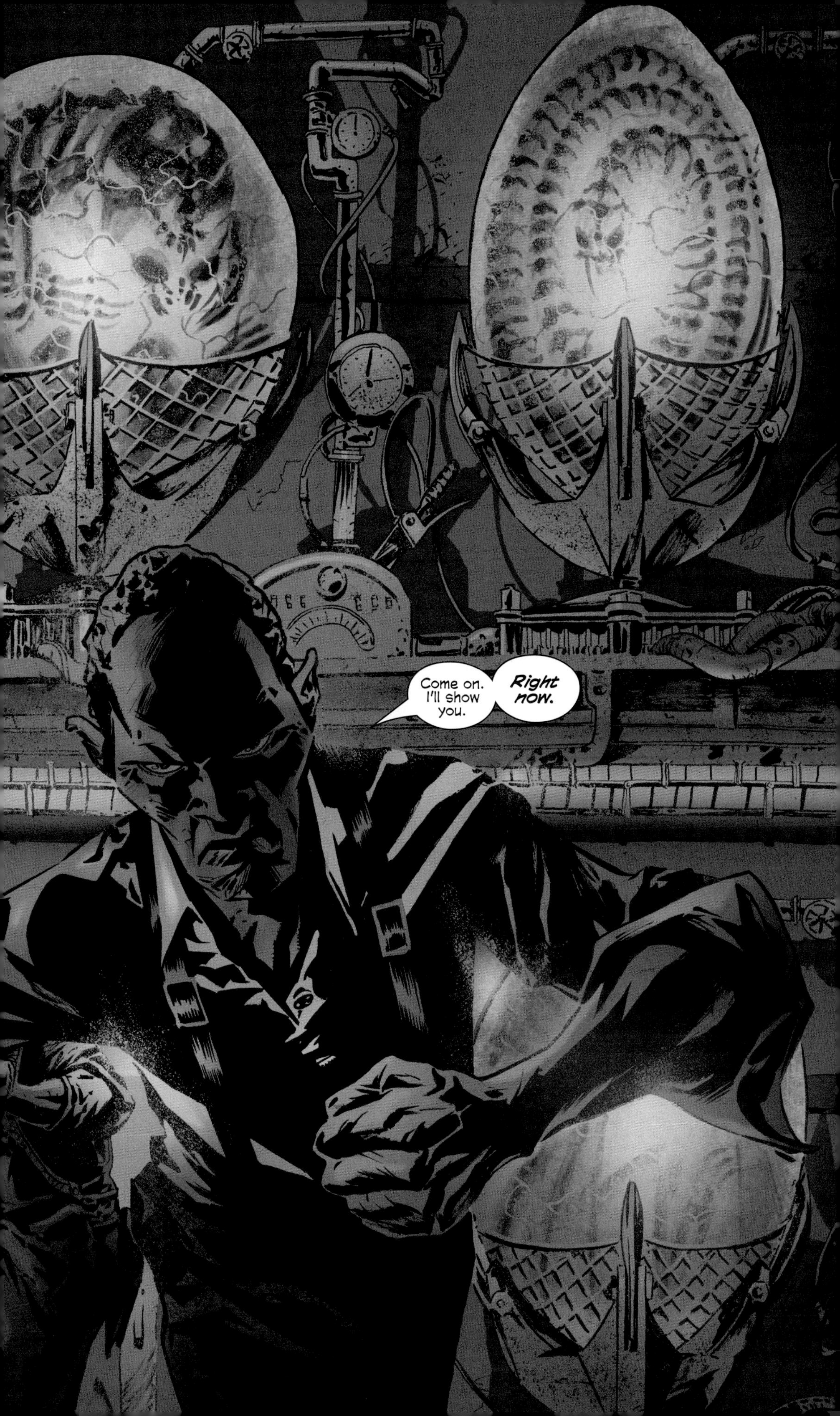
Come on. I'll show you.
Right now.

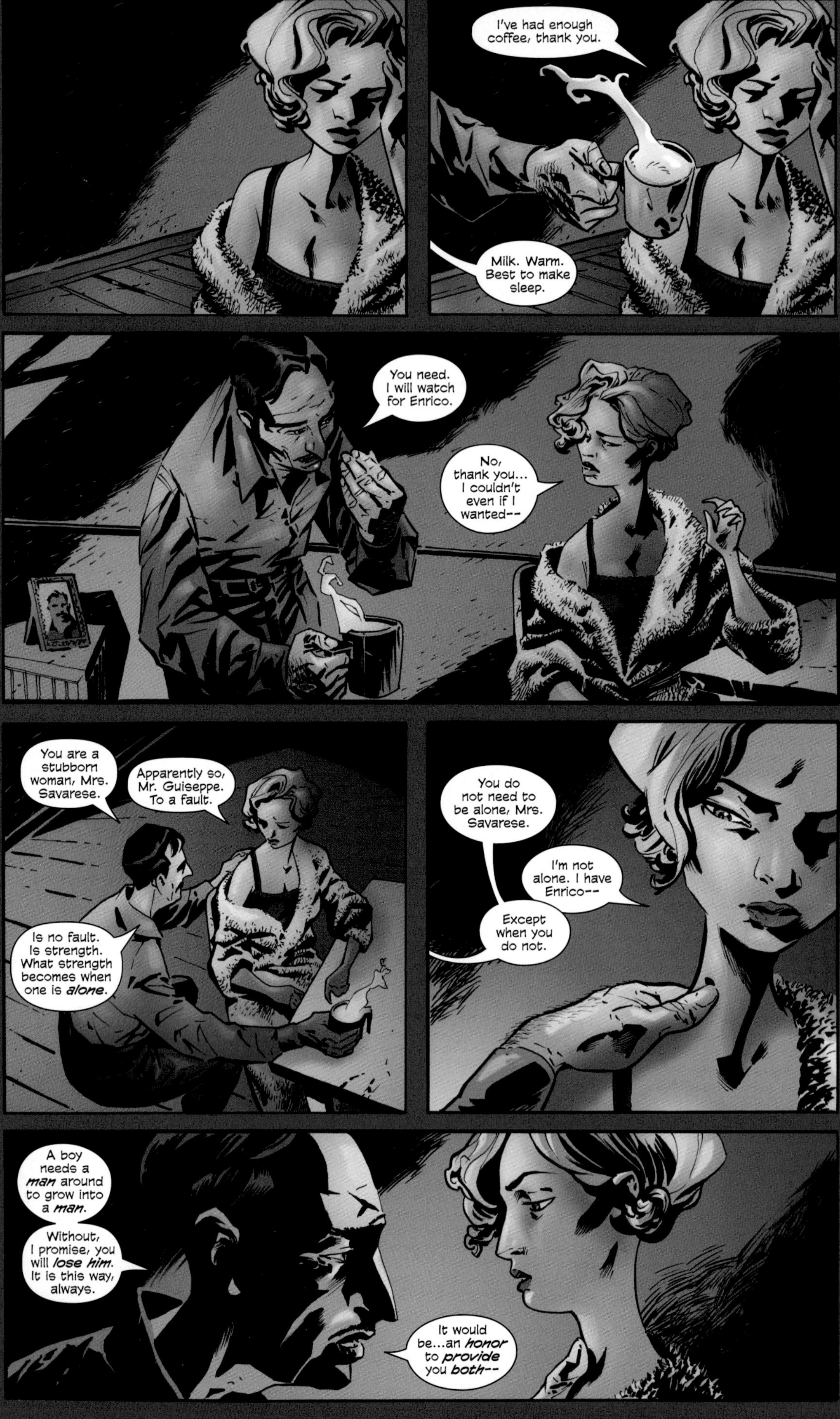
I've had enough coffee, thank you.
Milk. Warm. Best to make sleep.
You need. I will watch for Enrico.
No, thank you... I couldn't even if I wanted--
You are a stubborn woman, Mrs. Savarese.
Apparently so, Mr. Guiseppe. To a fault.
Is no fault. Is strength. What strength becomes when one is *alone*.
You do not need to be alone, Mrs. Savarese.
I'm not alone. I have Enrico--
Except when you do not.
A boy needs a *man* around to grow into a *man*.
Without, I promise, you will *lose him*. It is this way, always.
It would be...an *honor* to *provide* you *both*--

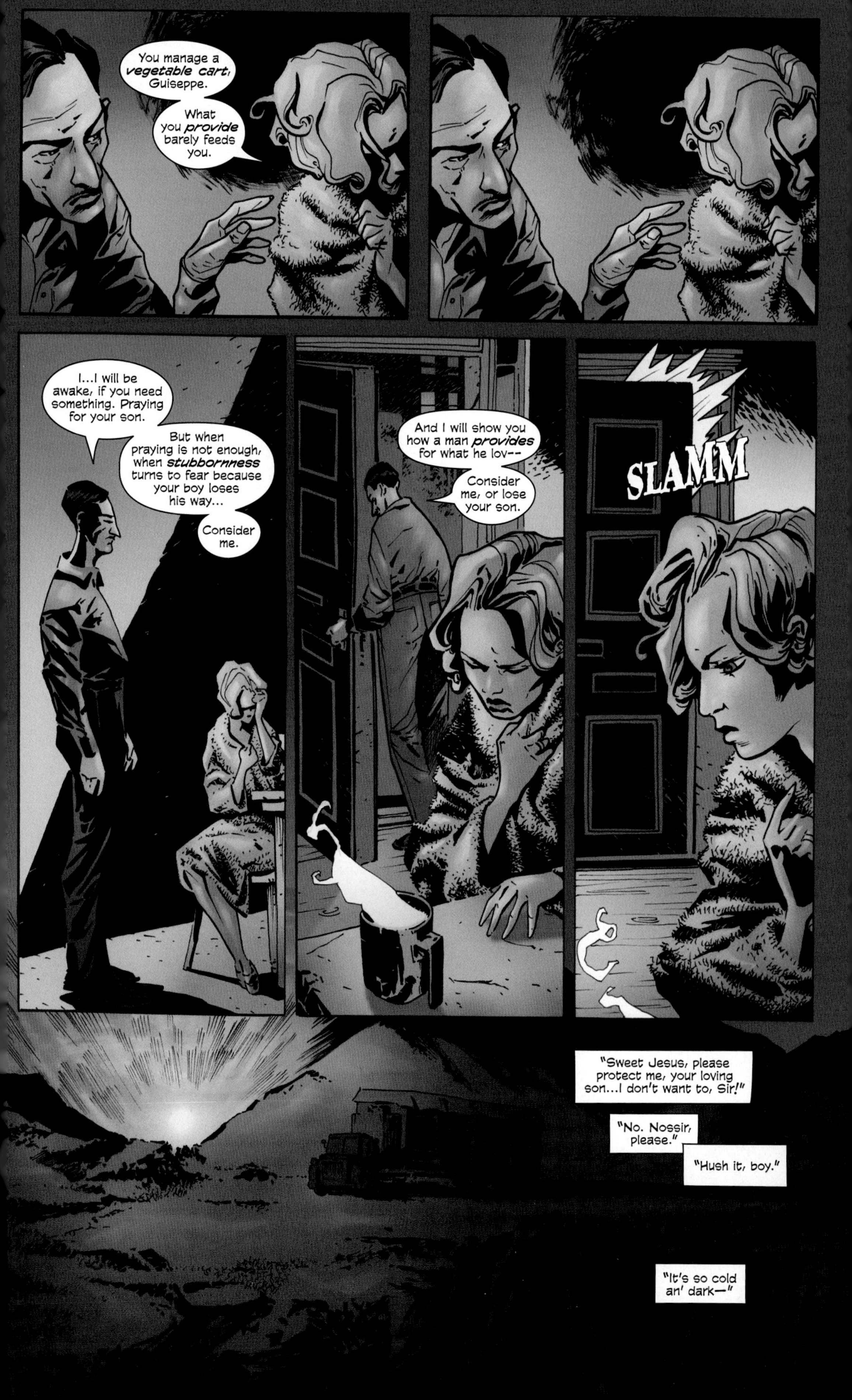

You manage a *vegetable cart*, Guiseppe.
What you *provide* barely feeds you.
I...I will be awake, if you need something. Praying for your son.
But when praying is not enough, when *stubbornness* turns to fear because your boy loses his way...
Consider me.
And I will show you how a man *provides* for what he lov--
Consider me, or lose your son.
SLAMM
"Sweet Jesus, please protect me, your loving son...I don't want to, Sir!"
"No. Nossir, please."
"Hush it, boy."
"It's so cold an' dark—"

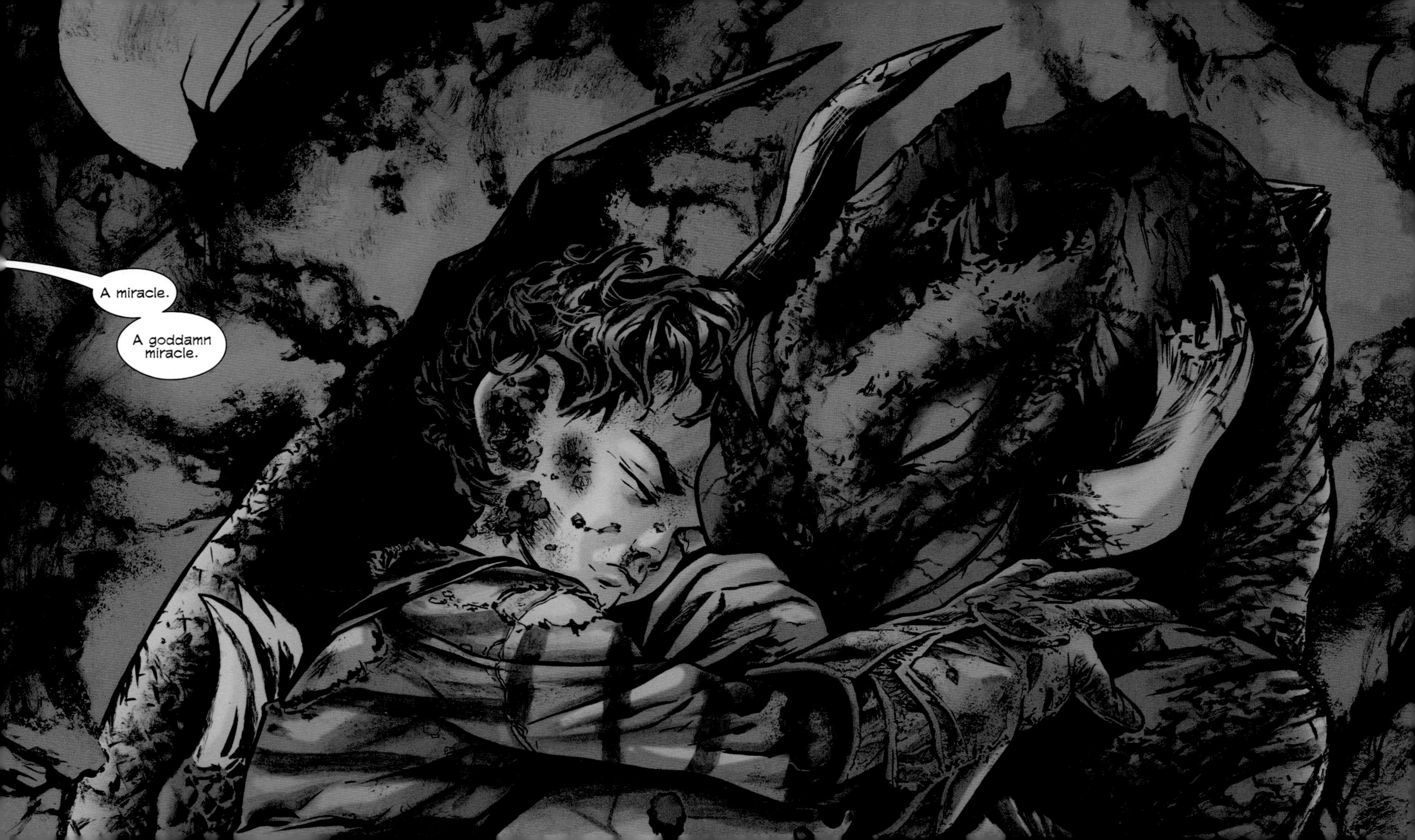
A miracle.
A goddamn miracle.

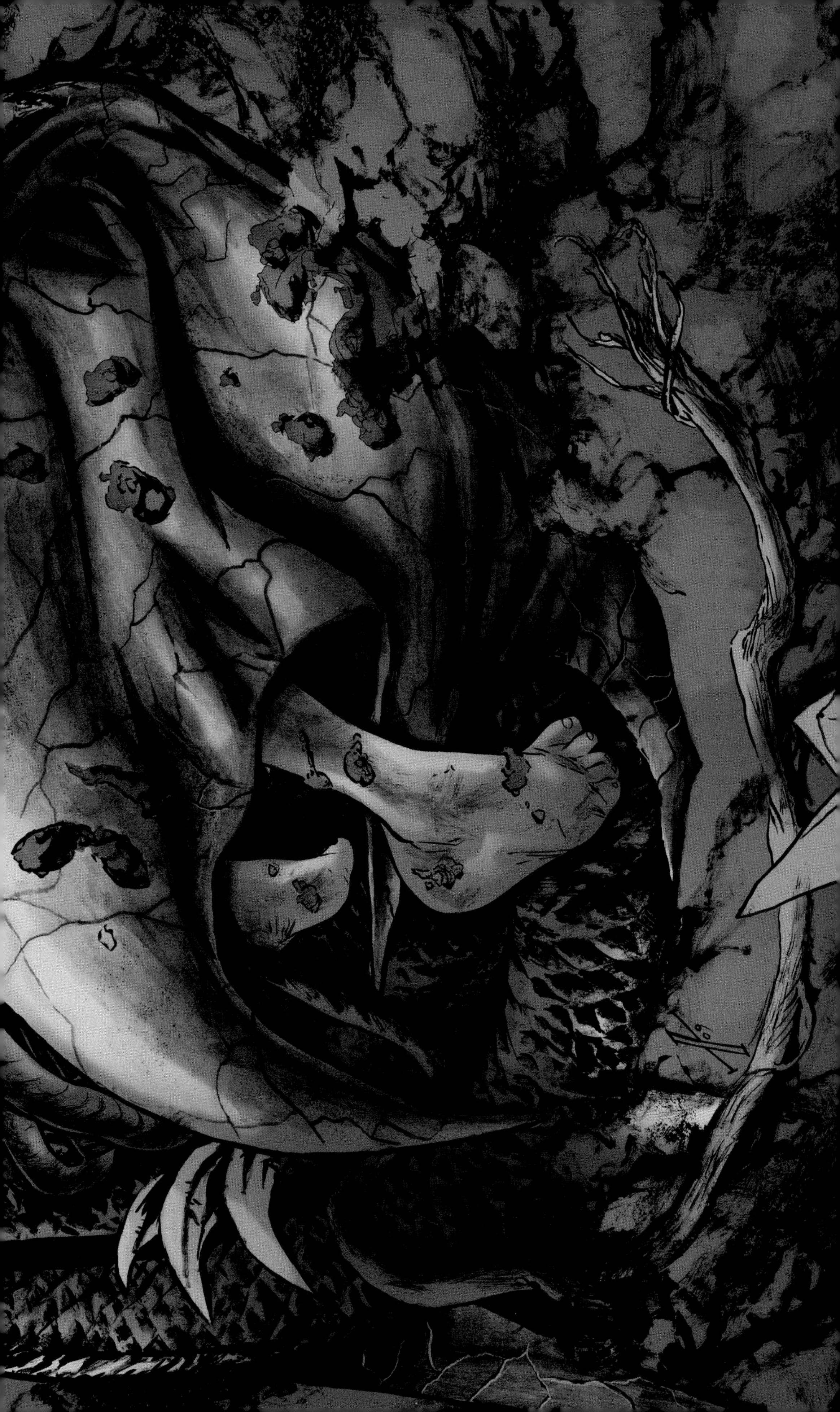

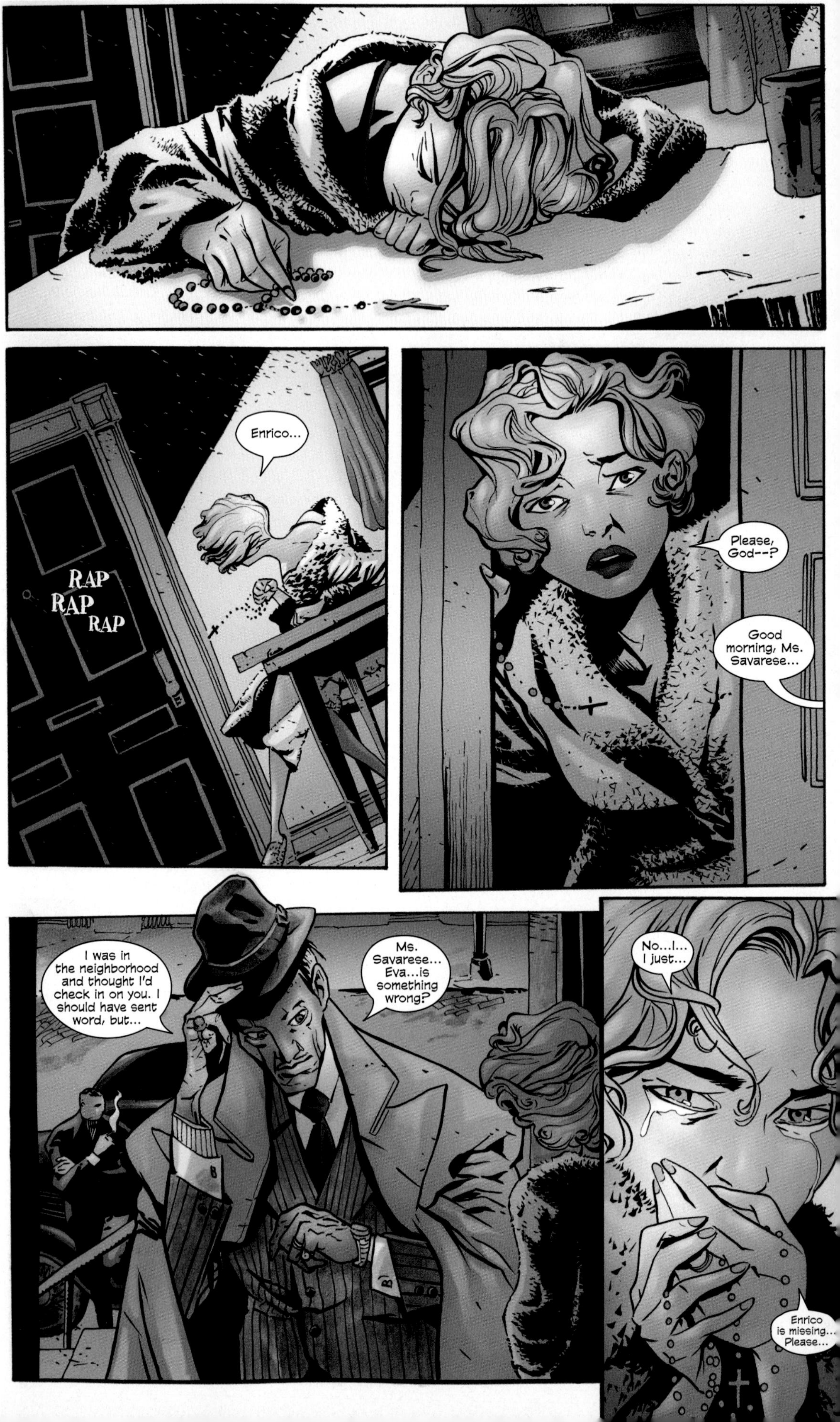
Enrico...
RAP
RAP
RAP
Please, God--?
Good morning, Ms. Savarese...
I was in the neighborhood and thought I'd check in on you. I should have sent word, but...
Ms. Savarese... Eva...is something wrong?
No...I... I just...
Enrico is missing... Please...

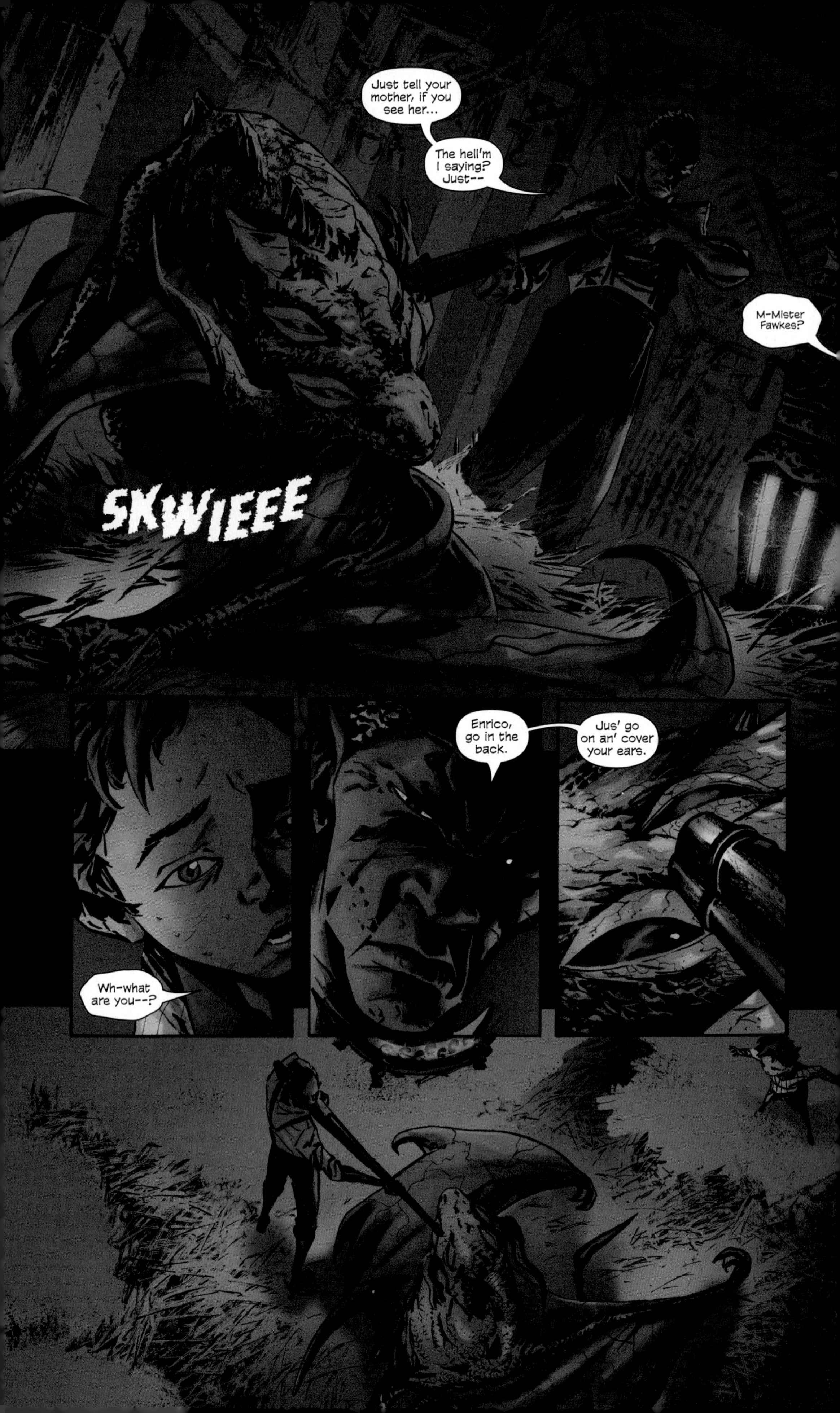
Just tell your mother, if you see her...
The hell'm I saying? Just--
M-Mister Fawkes?
SKWIEEE
Wh-what are you--?
Enrico, go in the back.
Jus' go on an' cover your ears.

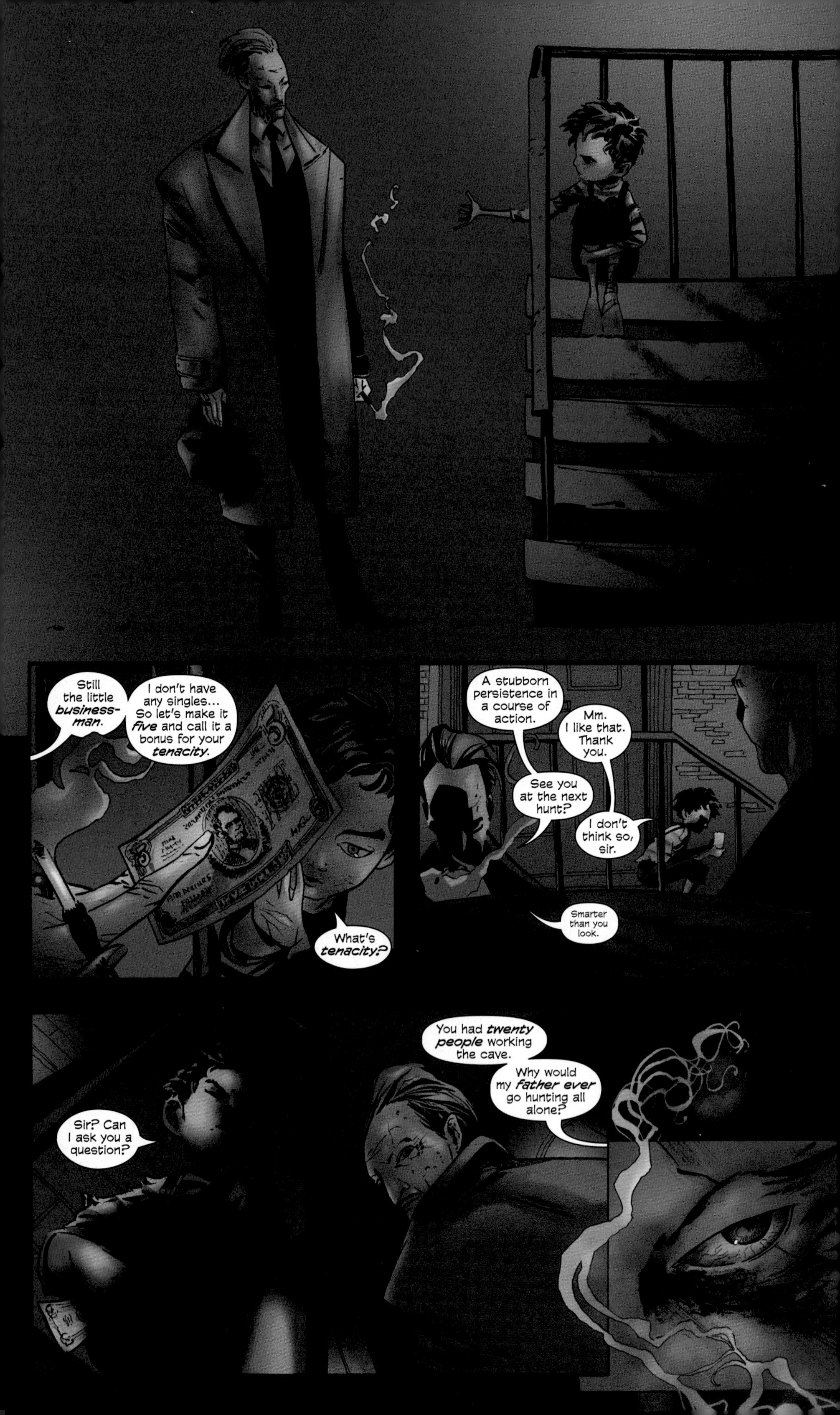
Still the little *business-man*.
I don't have any singles... So let's make it *five* and call it a bonus for your *tenacity*.
What's *tenacity?*
A stubborn persistence in a course of action.
Mm. I like that. Thank you.
See you at the next hunt?
I don't think so, sir.
Smarter than you look.
Sir? Can I ask you a question?
You had *twenty people* working the cave.
Why would my *father ever* go hunting all alone?

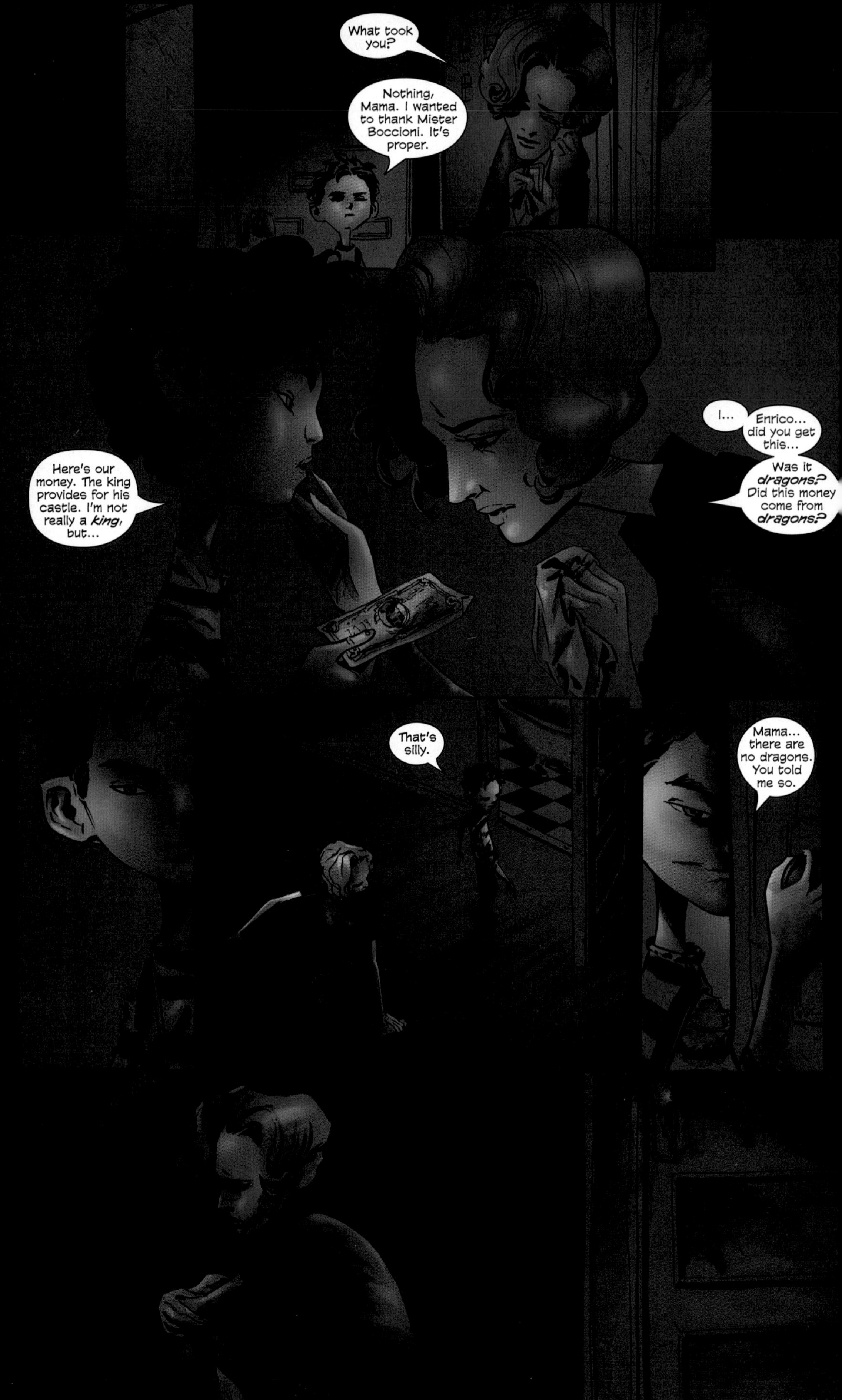
What took you?
Nothing, Mama. I wanted to thank Mister Boccioni. It's proper.
Here's our money. The king provides for his castle. I'm not really a *king*, but...
I...
Enrico... did you get this...
Was it *dragons?* Did this money come from *dragons?*
That's silly.
Mama... there are no dragons. You told me so.

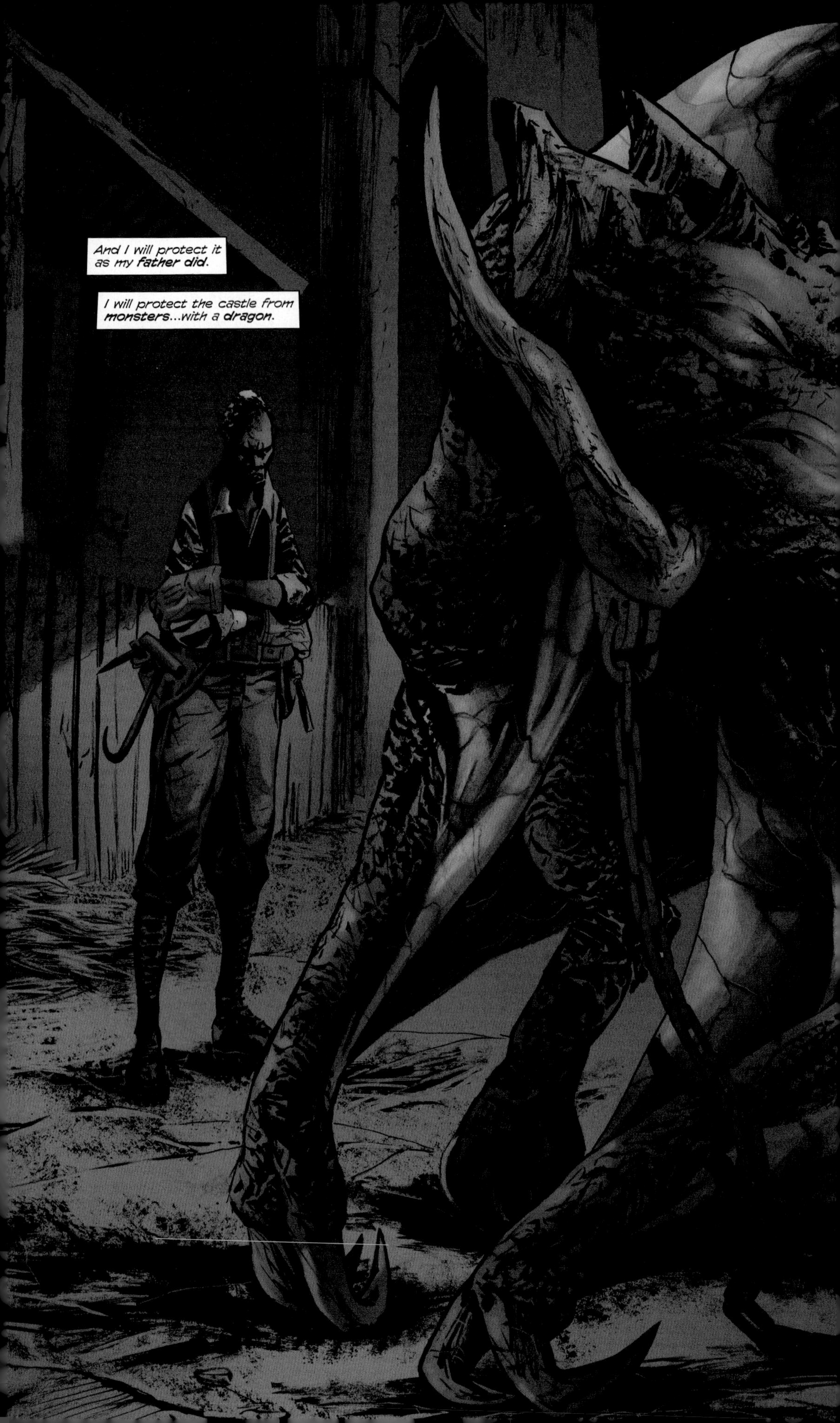
And I will protect it as my **father did**.
I will protect the castle from **monsters**...with a **dragon**.

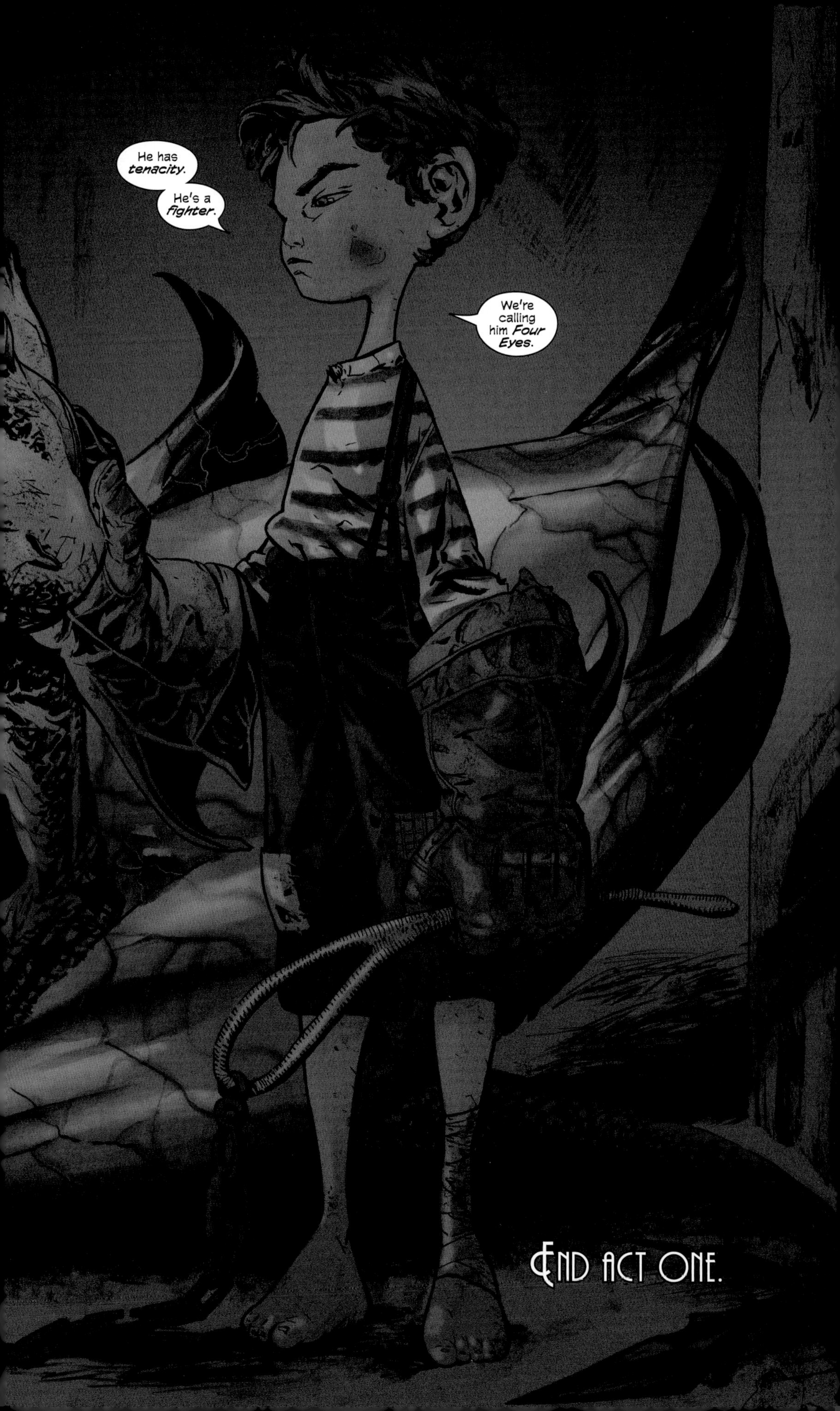
He has *tenacity*.
He's a *fighter*.
We're calling him *Four Eyes*.
End act one.

Big Burners Busted!

Borough of Richmond, New York

This Saturday, local and state authorities conducted a daring joint raid on a dragon fighting operation set in an abandoned stone quarry on Staten Island. Fifty Peace Officers took part in the maneuver, resulting in the arrest of over thirty poachers, trainers, and fight organizers. Nearly twenty-five thousand dollars in "house money" set to back illegal wagers was confiscated. The raid was a cooperative effort by Sergeant Russell Fitzgerald of the Richmond Police Department, and Sergeant Anthony Tabone of the New York State Troopers.

According to eyewitness accounts, the initial assault on the quarry went off without any bloodshed. However, the night turned deadly when one of the dragon handlers removed the protective blind from a primed bluefin and turned it loose on the officers. Bluefins are "primed" when they ingest the minimum amount of coal needed to exhale flames in combat. Five officers were burned to death before the beast could be destroyed.

This barbaric "sport" of dragon fighting has been on the rise in New York since the turn of the century when seemingly sterile dragon populations began breeding again, confounding biologists and dracospecialists alike. Though an underground phenomena, the spectacle has captured the imagination of many Americans seeking relief from the drudgery of these troubled times. Betting on dragon matches is rampant, especially in our poorest neighborhoods.

When questioned by a reporter for the Star about allegations that both state and local police are bribed to "turn a blind eye" to dragon fighting, Sgt. Fitzgerald became noticeably agitated. "We lost five men before the beast went down. Why don't you go ask their widows if they were on the take?" The remainder of the sergeant's comment cannot be printed in this article for concerns of decency.

Dracospecialists insist that Dragons are relatively harmless and have no interest in human beings when left to their own. They often quote a dubious statistic that there have been fewer than eighty unprovoked dragon attacks reported worldwide in the last half century. Dragons of every breed are considered "endangered species" and it is illegal to own, train, or fight them. Once a dragon has been taken from its natural habitat and "trained" for combat in the ring, federal law requires its destruction as it has proven impossible to release the creatures back into the wild without endangering human lives.

Announcing an evening of majestic brutality and incomparable sportsmanship!

An exhibition of the "Sport of Emperors" is to be conducted this September the 24th
including four undercard battles and one title match!

Thrill to the gladiatorial mastery of "Darwin's Darlings" as five different species
of dragons clash for supremacy before your very eyes!

Bouts Start At 10:00 P.M. Standard Time

TITLE BOUT:
Maximus Class   60-Unlimited ft.
The Old Man (BF)   *vs.*   True Emperor (Go)

UNDERCARD:
Tiberius Class   10-18 ft.
Gail's Fortune (BF)   *vs.*   Fang and Claw (BF)

Augustus Class   19-25 ft.
The Little Emperor (BF)   *vs.*   The Great Wall (Y)

Imperator Class   25-39 ft.
D'amato's Glory (A)   *vs.*   Mucho Gusto (Gi)

Caesar Class   40-55 ft.
Casey's Bat (BF)   *vs.*   Yellow Menace (Y)

Admission: 25 cents   (TAX INCLUDED)

Wagers begin at 5 cents

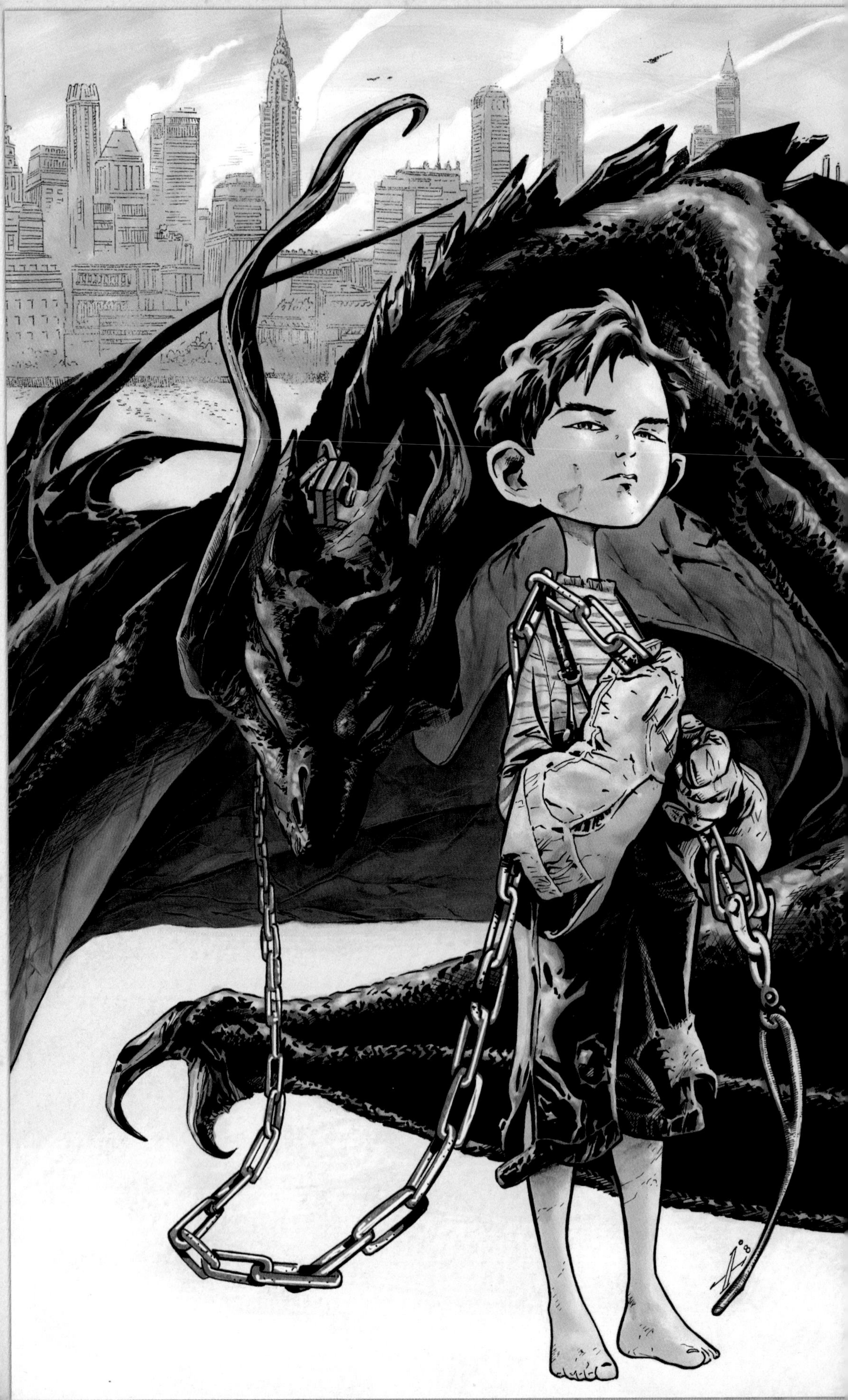

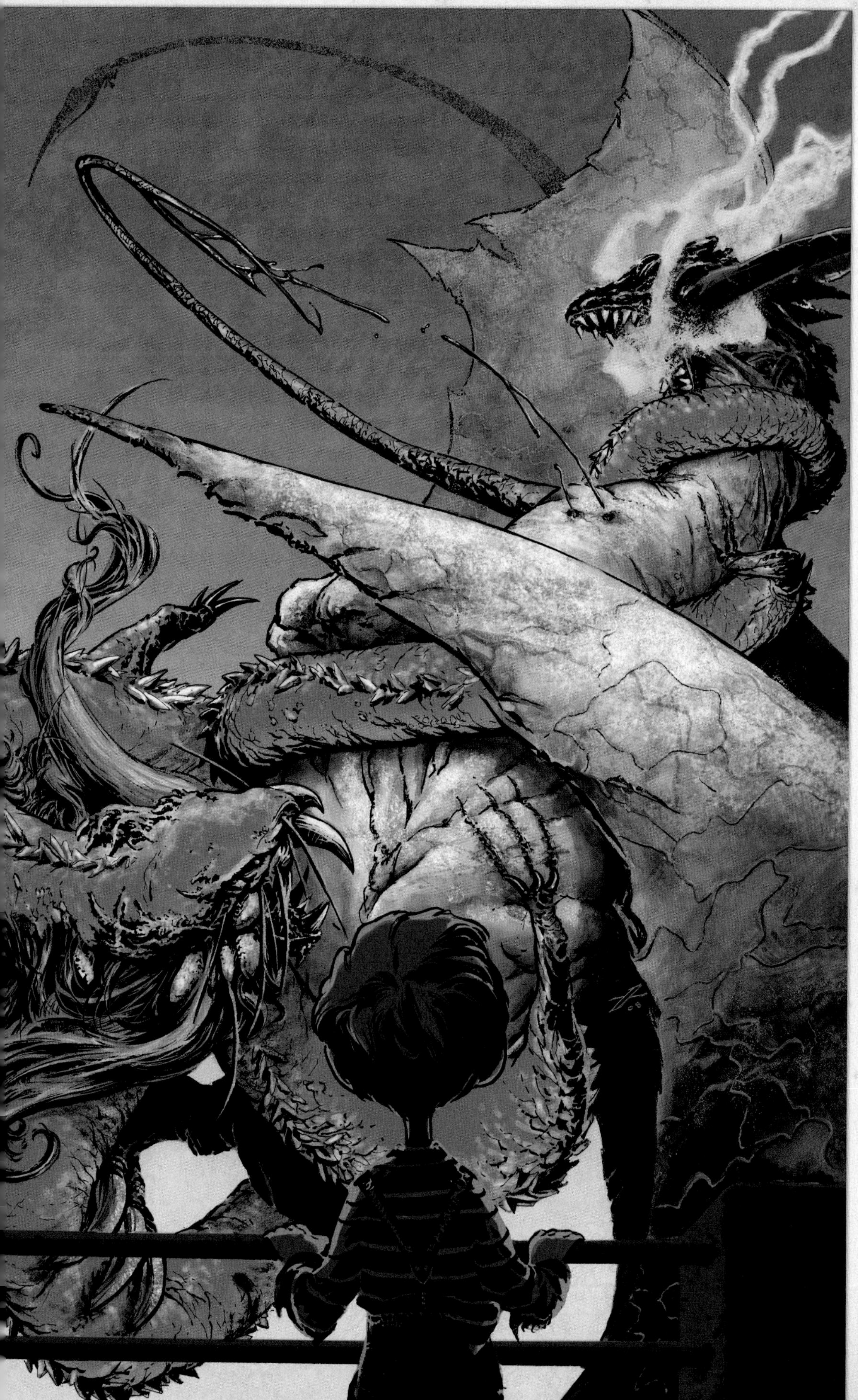

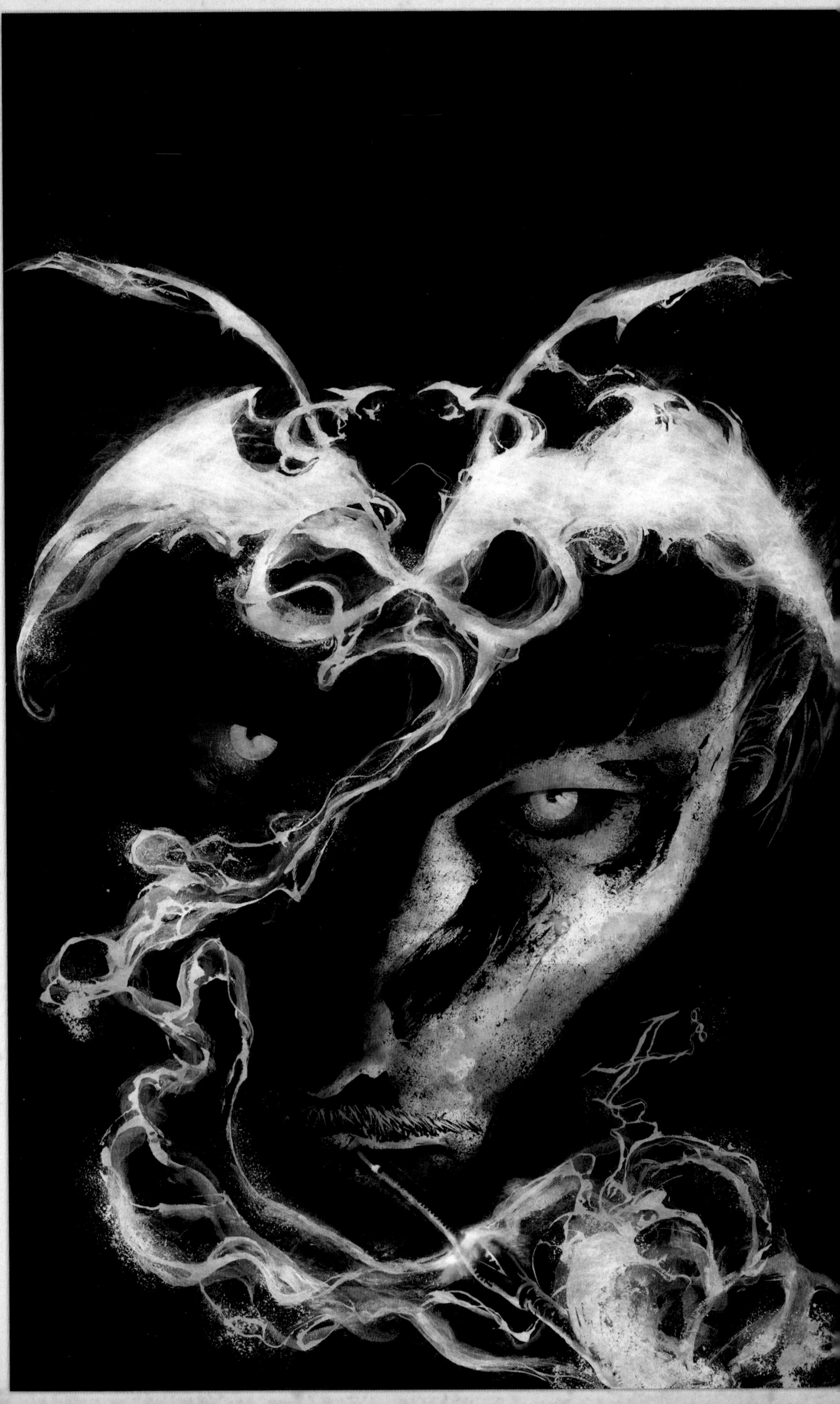

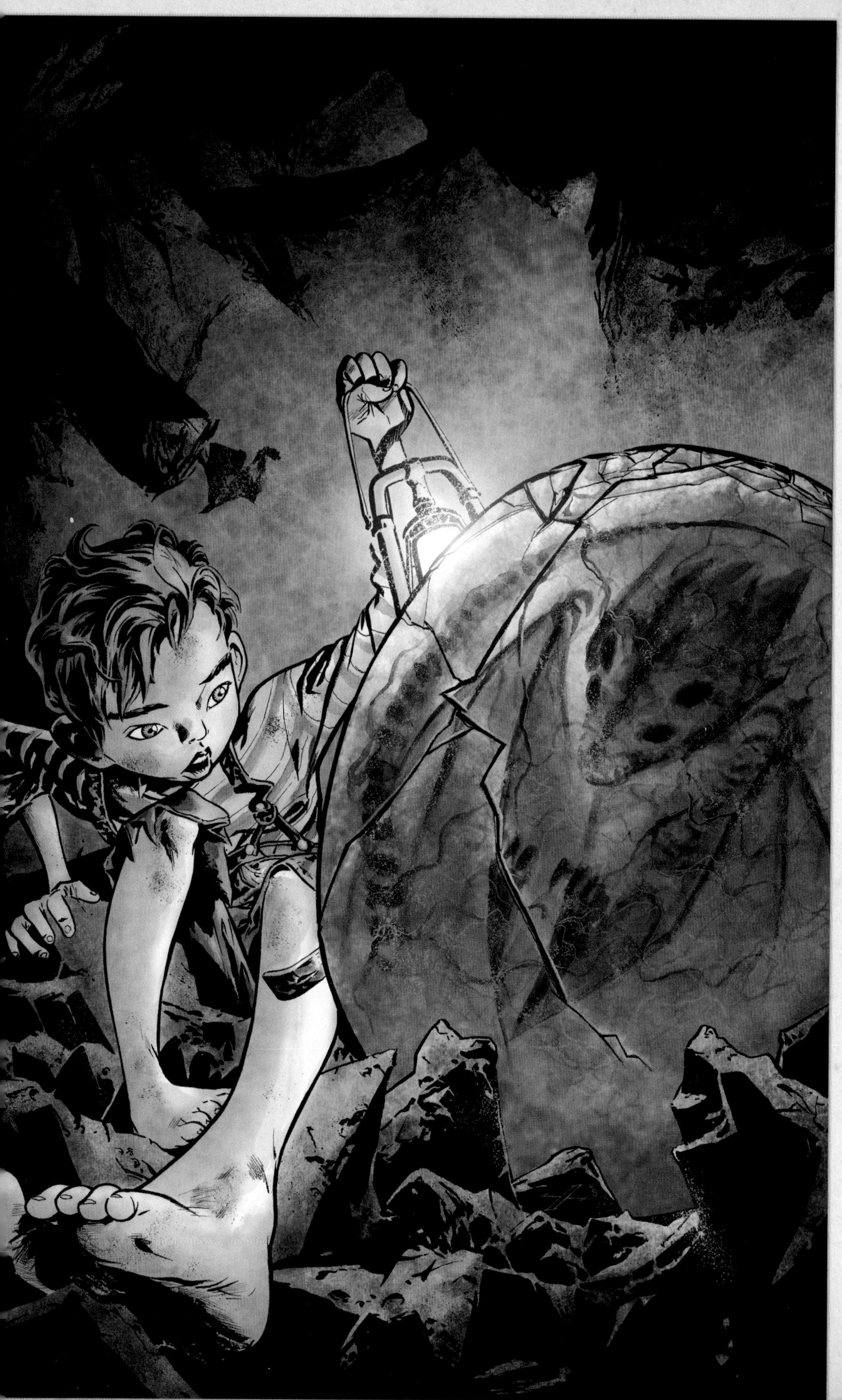

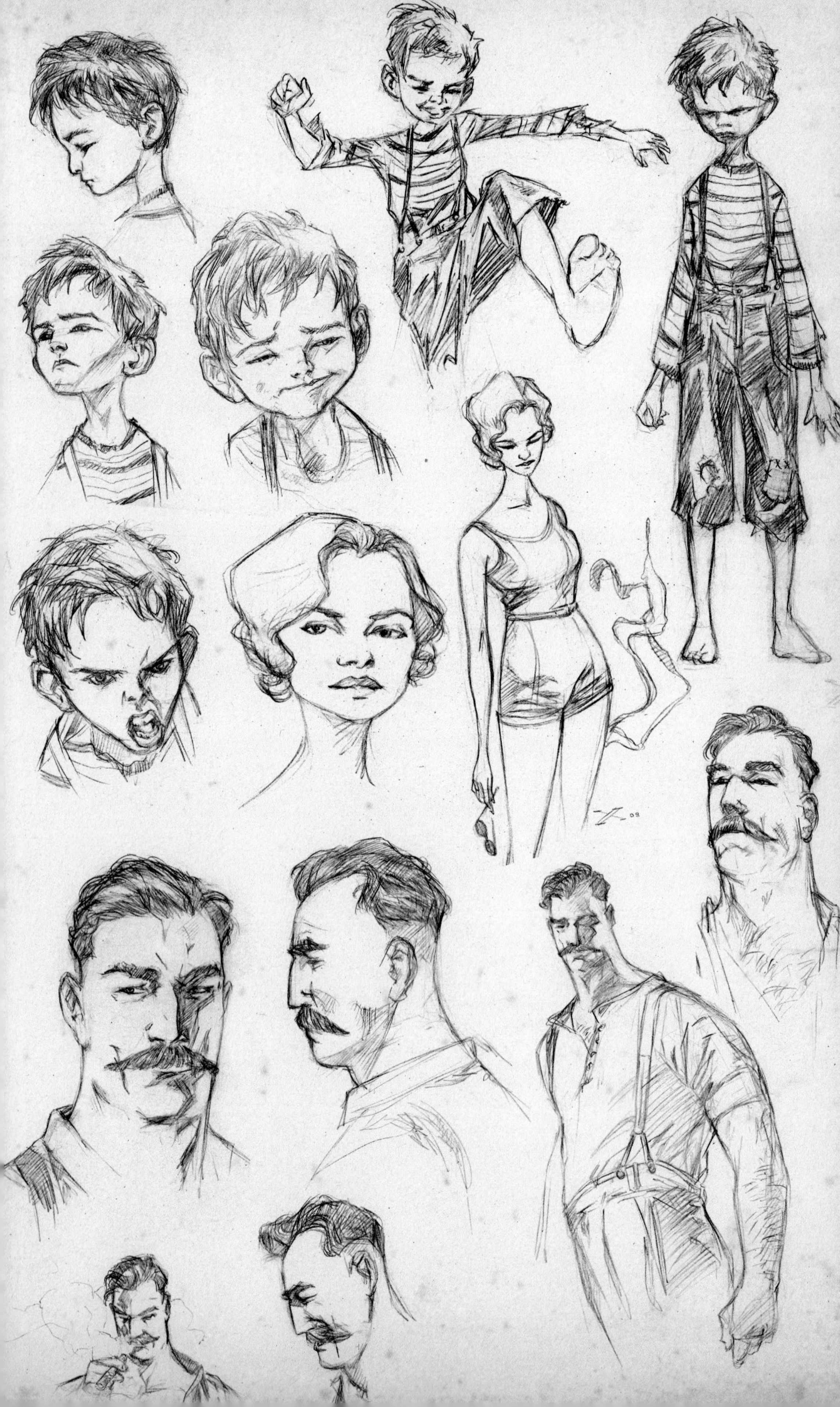

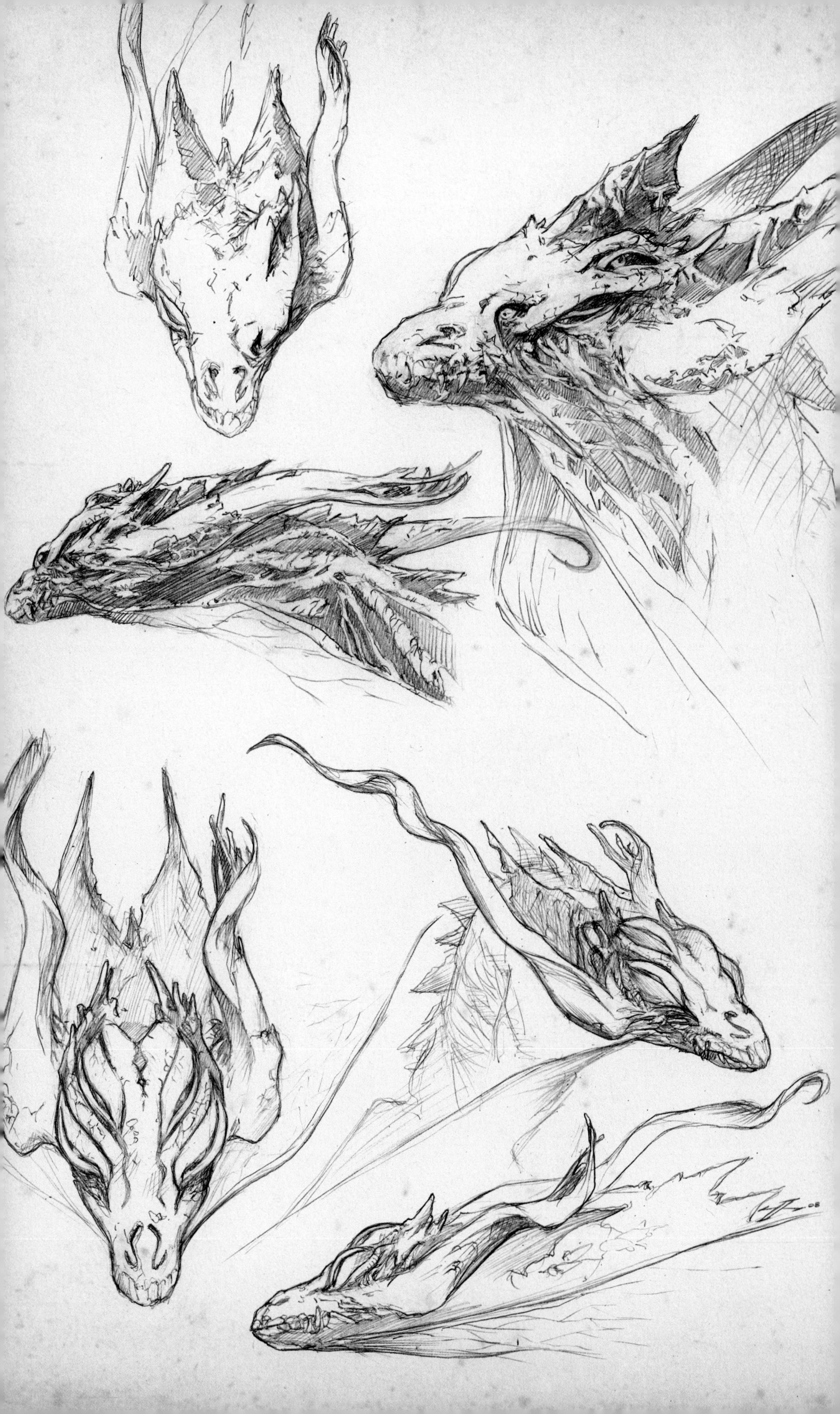

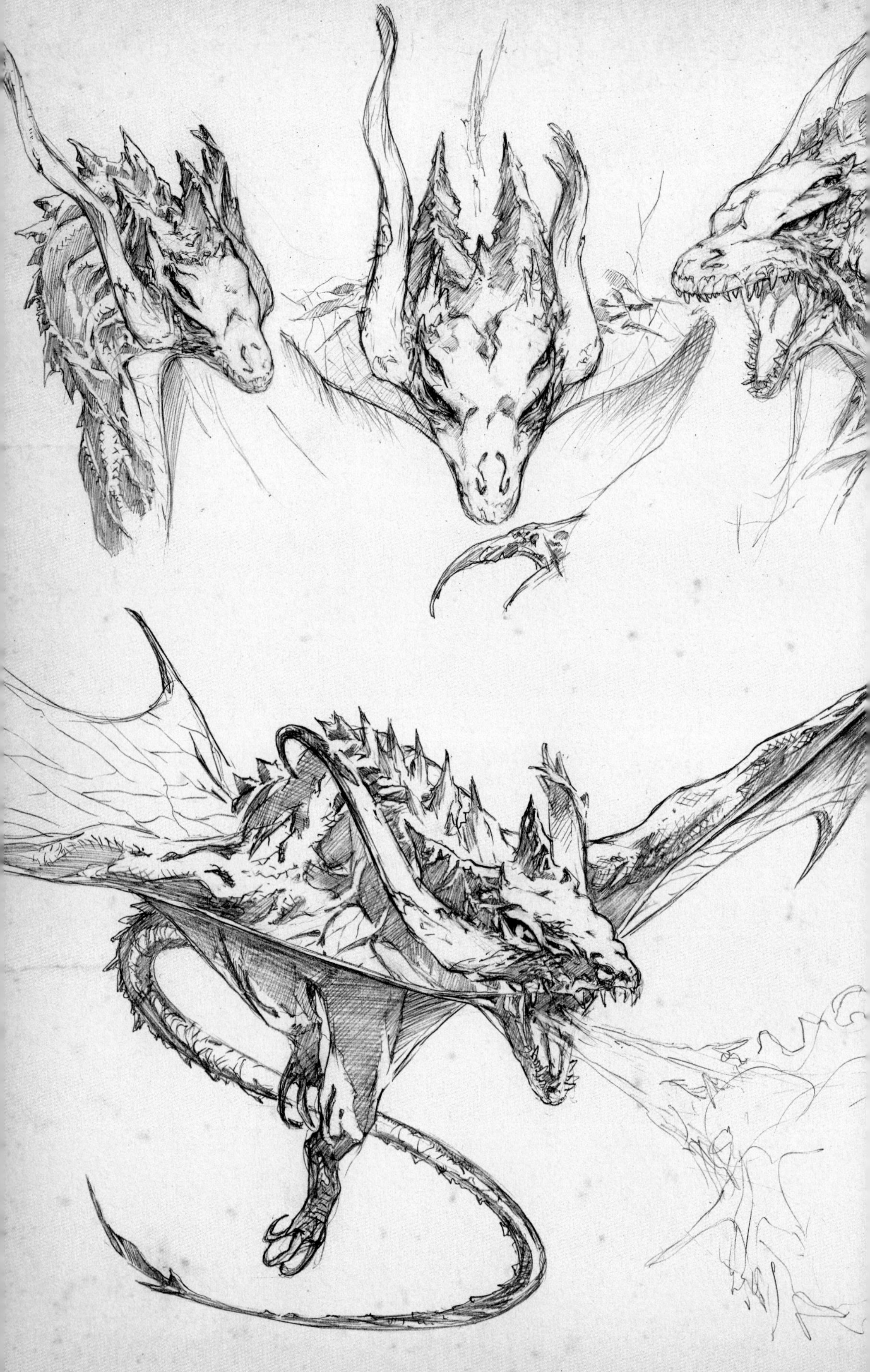